THE BEETLESS' GARDENING BOOK

An Organic Gardening Songbook / Guidebook

Containing the poetry of Jam Lemon, Pear Machete,
Joychoi Heirloom, and Rutabaga Variety --
four lads who made organic gardening
a household word once more

Edited and Annotated by Chris Roth

Foreword by Alan Kapuler, Ph.D.
Research Director, Seeds of Change

Carrotseed Press
Cottage Grove, OR
1997

THE BEETLESS' GARDENING BOOK:
An Organic Gardening Songbook / Guidebook
Copyright © 1997 by Chris Roth

First Printing: 1997

ISBN 0-9657090-2-7

Library of Congress Catalog Card Number: 97-91588

Manufactured in the United States of America by McNaughton & Gunn.
Printed on acid-free, recycled paper using soy-based inks.

No part of this book may be reproduced in any form or by any electronic or mechanical means, including information storage and retrieval systems, without permission in writing from the publisher, except by a reviewer who may quote brief passages in a review.

Front cover design by Meera Subramanian and Steve Colbert.

All Beetless poems Copyright © 1997 Chris Roth
except I'M EATING GOOD FOOD, WE CAN TURN IT 'ROUND,
Copyright © 1997 Larry Dobberstein.

For copyright information on the songs which form the background to these poems, see p. 4.

Additional copies ($10.95 postpaid), and bulk discounts available.
Carrotseed Press • PO Box 1174 • Cottage Grove, OR 97424 • USA
(541)942-8198

Publisher's Cataloging-in-Publication

Roth, Chris.
    The Beetless' Gardening Book: An Organic Gardening Songbook/Guidebook / by Chris Roth.
    112 p. 22 cm.
    Includes bibliographical references and index.
    ISBN 0-9657090-2-7 (pbk.: acid-free paper): $8.95
    1. Organic gardening. 2. Gardening. 3. Agriculture.
4. Humorous poetry. 5. Verse satire. 6. Music -- Humor. I. Title.
SB453.5.R68 1997
635.0484   97-91588

DISCLAIMER: ON THE BEETLESS' POETIC LICENSE

In the tradition of Walt Whitman's *Song of Myself*, the "songs" in *The Beetless' Gardening Book* are *not*, in fact, songs *per se*, but poems. They are intended to sound particularly good when read or recited to a background of the specified Beatles tunes, but the idea that they are "songs" themselves is merely a fiction, a gimmick, a metaphor, part of the satire.

This distinction is important because, while no-one can "own" the meter of a poem, the tunes of songs can be (and are) owned and protected by copyright. While written parodies, in verse form, are considered acceptable free speech, permission is required to record or publicly perform any copyrighted musical work, especially if it is given new lyrics. The current owners of the copyrights on the Beatles' songs do not allow any changes to the original lyrics in recordings or public performances.

Therefore, these poems may be used for private and small group amusement -- you may even find yourself modulating your pitch a bit as you read them -- but they may not be legally performed in any setting to which the general public has access (e.g. coffee houses, concert halls, football stadiums), nor recorded and offered to the public in any form (cd, vinyl, audio or video tape, etc.). Moreover, they are not intended as a substitute or competition for the music which inspired them. The Beetless strongly urge you to purchase all of the original Beatles albums which contain the background songs, listed on pp. 59 and 83.

Sorry to start out on such a heavy note (sounds like E-flat to our ears). We just don't want you (or ourselves) to get sued. The tone lightens up from here on out. We promise.

Thanks to the poetic license and good taste with which they pepper their work, the Beetless have brought joy to the world without causing anyone harm or legal agony. We owe them a debt of gratitude. Hats off!

Beatles Music Copyrights

All the original music and lyrics which form the intended backdrop for these Beetless poems were formerly Copyright © 1963 to 1970 Northern Songs Ltd., and are currently Copyright © Sony/ATV Songs LLC, all rights controlled and administered by EMI Blackwood Music Inc., under license from Sony/ATV Songs LLC, (BMI) all rights reserved, international copyright secured, except:
LONG TALL SALLY Copyright © 1956 Venice Music Inc., USA
LOVE ME DO Copyright © 1962 MPL Communications
PLEASE PLEASE ME Copyright © 1962 Dick James Music Ltd.
MISTER MOONLIGHT Copyright © 1964 Lowery Music Company Inc., USA
PIGGIES Copyright © 1968 Harrisongs Ltd.
OCTOPUS'S GARDEN Copyright © 1969 Startling Music Ltd.
HERE COMES THE SUN Copyright © 1969 Harrisongs Ltd.
and from the "Beetless Bootleg" section:
ROLL OVER BEETHOVEN Copyright © 1956 Arc Music Corp., USA
ROCK AND ROLL MUSIC Copyright © 1957 Arc Music Corp., USA
SLOW DOWN Copyright © 1957 ATV Music Ltd.
WORDS OF LOVE Copyright © 1957 MPL Communications Inc.
P.S. I LOVE YOU Copyright © 1962 MPL Communications Inc.
SAVOY TRUFFLE, WHILE MY GUITAR GENTLY WEEPS Copyright © 1968 Harrisongs Ltd.

Acknowledgements and Dedication

Thanks to the many people who encouraged me (sometimes unwittingly) to write and publish this book, including:

Interns, visitors, staff, and friends of Aprovecho Research Center, where I first encountered many of these experiences and perspectives

The farmers and gardeners I have worked with, in various settings, over the past dozen or so years, for helping me along this path

Friends in Eugene and elsewhere, who helped keep me sane and on this path even when they couldn't fathom it

Those whose enthusiastic response to this book's rough draft, and willingness to put their names on the line in its praise (see back cover), have brought it into print

Larry, Mushroom, Meera, and Steve, for their special contributions

Michael I., Patrick S., and others who encouraged my interest in the Beatles at an early age

John, Paul, George, and Ringo, for the savoy truffles and cranberry sauce

Teachers, friends, and others who told me I'd write a book someday; this is probably not what they anticipated

The librarians, college employees, and those in the book trade who aided me at critical stages in this book's final preparation, and helped initiate me into the world of publishing

A certain large mountain in Northern California, in whose shadow the Beetless were born

And especially to my musical (and also literary, and more-or-less down-to-earth) family of origin -- Mother, Dad, and Michael -- who lent me not only their computer, advice, and technical support, but also their tolerance, encouragement, and love -- and to whom this book is dedicated.

CONTENTS
(- Small numbers refer to page #s -)
LARGE NUMBERS REFER TO POEM #s

(- 9 -) **FOREWORD**

(- 12 -) **INTRODUCTION**

(- 14 -) 1 **ACROSS THE SEED BEDS FIRST** (Music: ACROSS THE UNIVERSE, Lennon-McCartney)
(- 15 -) **LOST SONGS OF THE BEETLESS PT. 1** (#s 58-59)

(- 16 -) 2 **ALL YOUR SEEDS ARE LOVE** (Music: ALL YOU NEED IS LOVE, Lennon-McCartney)
(- 17 -) **LOST SONGS OF THE BEETLESS PT. 2** (#s 60-61)

(- 18 -) 3 **BUG ME DO** (Music: LOVE ME DO, Lennon-McCartney)
(- 19 -) 4 **CARRY THAT CRATE** (Music: CARRY THAT WEIGHT, Lennon-McCartney)
(- 19 -) **LOST SONGS OF THE BEETLESS PT. 3** (#62)

(- 20 -) 5 **CHICO, YOU'RE A DITCH MAN** (Music: BABY, YOU'RE A RICH MAN, Lennon-McCartney)
(- 21 -) **LOST SONGS OF THE BEETLESS PT. 4** (#s 63-65)

(- 22 -) 6 **DO YOU WANT TO KNOW THE SEED DEPTH?** (Music: DO YOU WANT TO KNOW A SECRET, Lennon-McCartney)
(- 23 -) 7 **EARTHWORM** (Music: BLACKBIRD, Lennon-McCartney)
(- 24 -) 8 **FIXING A TOOL** (Music: FIXING A HOLE, Lennon-McCartney)
(- 25 -) 9 **GOOD DAY SUNCHOKES** (Music: GOOD DAY SUNSHINE, Lennon-McCartney)
(- 26 -) 10 **GOPHER BITES** (Music: HOLD ME TIGHT, Lennon-McCartney)
(- 27 -) **LOST SONGS OF THE BEETLESS PT. 5** (#s 66-68)

(- 28 -) 11 **GOT TO PICK YOU, NOT USE A KNIFE** (Music: GOT TO GET YOU INTO MY LIFE, Lennon-McCartney)
(- 29 -) **LOST SONGS OF THE BEETLESS PT. 6** (#s 69-72)

(- 30 -) 12 **GRASSMAN** (Music: TAXMAN, Harrison)

(- 31 -) 13 **GREENS THAT ARE MUSTARDS** (Music: MEAN MR. MUSTARD, Lennon-McCartney)
(- 32 -) 14 **A HARD CLAY SOIL** (Music: A HARD DAY'S NIGHT, Lennon-McCartney)
(- 33 -) **LOST SONGS OF THE BEETLESS PT. 7** (#s 73-74)

(- 34 -) 15 **HERE COME THE SLUGS** (Music: HERE COMES THE SUN, Harrison)
(- 35 -) **LOST SONGS OF THE BEETLESS PT. 8** (#s 75-77)

(- 36 -) 16 **I SAW HERBS STANDING THERE** (Music: I SAW HER STANDING THERE, Lennon-McCartney)
(- 37 -) 17 **I TILL** (Music: I WILL, Lennon-McCartney)

(- 38 -) 18 **I WANNA FREEZE AND CAN** (Music: I WANNA BE YOUR MAN, Lennon-McCartney)
(- 39 -) **LOST SONGS OF THE BEETLESS PT. 9** (#s 78-80)

(- 40 -) 19 **I WANT TO DIG BY HAND** (Music: I WANT TO HOLD YOUR HAND, Lennon-McCartney)
(- 41 -) **LOST SONGS OF THE BEETLESS PT. 10** (#s 81-82)

(- 42 -) 20 **I WANT TO SELL YOU** (Music: I WANT TO TELL YOU, Harrison)
(- 43 -) 21 **I'M A SHROOMER** (Music: I'M A LOSER, Lennon-McCartney)
(- 44 -) 22 **I'M EATING GOOD FOOD** (Music: I'M LOOKING THROUGH YOU, Lennon-McCartney)
(- 45 -) **MEET THE BEETLESS**

(- 46 -) 23 **IT'S ALL GOOD MULCH** (Music: IT'S ALL TOO MUCH, Harrison)

(- 47 -) **LOST SONGS OF THE BEETLESS PT. 11** (#s 83-85) **& PT. 12** (#s 86-87)
(- 48 -) 24 **I'VE GOT A SEEDLING** (Music: I'VE GOT A FEELING, Lennon-McCartney)
(- 49 -) **LOST SONGS OF THE BEETLESS PT. 13** (#88)

(- 50 -) 25 **I'VE JUST SEEN A FROST** (Music: I'VE JUST SEEN A FACE, Lennon-McCartney)
(- 51 -) **LOST SONGS OF THE BEETLESS PT. 14** (#s 89-90)

(- 52 -) 26 **I'VE JUST SEEN A PLACE** (Music: I'VE JUST SEEN A FACE, Lennon-McCartney)
(- 52 -) **LOST SONGS OF THE BEETLESS PT. 15** (#s 91-92)

(- 54 -) **LOST SONGS OF THE BEETLESS PT. 16** (#s 93-95)

(- 55 -) 27 **THE LONG ERODED PATH** (Music: THE LONG AND WINDING ROAD, Lennon-McCartney)
(- 56 -) 28 **LOOSELY FIRM THE EDGES OF SEEDFLATS** (Music: LUCY IN THE SKY WITH DIAMONDS, Lennon-McCartney)
(- 57 -) **LOST SONGS OF THE BEETLESS PT. 17** (#s 96-97)

(- 58 -) 29 **LUCKY STIFFS, THEIR LAND IS PAID** (Music: LOVELY RITA, Lennon-McCartney)
(- 59 -) **THE MUSIC OF THE BEATLES: CROSS-REFERENCED ALBUM LIST**
(- 60 -) 30 **MAXWELL'S PLASTIC BUCKET** (Music: MAXWELL'S SILVER HAMMER, Lennon-McCartney)
(- 61 -) **LOST SONGS OF THE BEETLESS PT. 18** (#s 98-99)

(- 62 -) 31 **MIGUEL** (Music: MICHELLE, Lennon-McCartney)

(- 63 -) **GARDENING WITH THE BEETLESS: QUIZ #1**

(- 64 -) 32 **MISTER PRUNE-RIGHT** (Music: MISTER MOONLIGHT, Roy Lee Johnson)

(- 65 -) 33 MOTHER NATURE'S WON (Music: MOTHER NATURE'S SON, Lennon-McCartney)
(- 66 -) 34 MULCH! (Music: HELP!, Lennon-McCartney)

(- 67 -) GARDENING WITH THE BEETLESS: QUIZ #2

(- 68 -) 35 OH! BARLEY (Music: OH! DARLING, Lennon-McCartney)
(- 69 -) 36 ONE AFTER WEST TWENTY-NINE (Music: ONE AFTER NINE-O-NINE, Lennon-McCartney)
(- 70 -) 37 PAPERBACK MULCHER (Music: PAPERBACK WRITER, Lennon-McCartney)
(- 71 -) LOST SONGS OF THE BEETLESS PT. 19 (#100)

(- 72 -) 38 PERMACULTURE GARDEN (Music: OCTOPUS'S GARDEN, Richard Starkey)
(- 73 -) ANSWERS TO BEETLESS GARDENING QUIZZES

(- 74 -) 39 PLEASE WEED ME (Music: PLEASE PLEASE ME, Lennon-McCartney)
(- 75 -) 40 PREPPING DAY (Music: YESTERDAY, Lennon-McCartney)
(- 76 -) 41 PVC PAM (Music: POLYTHENE PAM, Lennon-McCartney)
(- 77 -) 42 RAINBIRD (Music: RAIN, Lennon-McCartney)

(- 78 -) 43 ROCK DUSTING SOON (Music: ROCKY RACCOON, Lennon-McCartney)
(- 80 -) 44 SALT AND PEPPER'S ONLY FOR WHEN VEGETABLES ARE BLAND (Music: SGT. PEPPER'S LONELY HEARTS CLUB BAND, Lennon-McCartney)
(- 81 -) 45 SHE DUG YOU (Music: SHE LOVES YOU, Lennon-McCartney)
(- 82 -) 46 SHE SAID RAISED BED (Music: SHE SAID SHE SAID, Lennon-McCartney)
(- 83 -) THE BEATLES: PERENNIALS (ADDITIONAL ALBUMS)

(- 84 -) 47 SHE SAID SHE COMPOSTED IN WINDROWS (Music: SHE CAME IN THROUGH THE BATHROOM WINDOW, Lennon-McCartney)
(- 85 -) 48 SHORT ON SALARY (Music: LONG TALL SALLY, Enotris Johnson, Richard Penniman, Robert Blackwell)
(- 86 -) 49 THINNINGS (Music: PIGGIES, Harrison)

(- 87 -) 50 THE TURD (Music: THE WORD, Lennon-McCartney)

(- 88 -) 51 TWELVE MONTHS A YEAR (Music: EIGHT DAYS A WEEK, Lennon-McCartney)
(- 90 -) 52 WE CAN TURN IT 'ROUND (Music: WE CAN WORK IT OUT, Lennon-McCartney)
(- 91 -) 53 WHY DON'T WE DO IT WITHOUT ROADS? (Music: WHY DON'T WE DO IT IN THE ROAD?, Lennon-McCartney)
(- 92 -) 54 WORKDAY (Music: BIRTHDAY, Lennon-McCartney)

(- 93 -) **BIBLIOGRAPHY / RESOURCES PT. 1**

(- 94 -) 55 YOU NEVER LEND ME YOUR CRUMMY (Music: YOU NEVER GIVE ME YOUR MONEY, Lennon-McCartney)
(- 94 -) **THE BEETLESS VS. THE ROLLING SCONES?**

(- 96 -) 56 YOU WON'T SEED ME (Music: YOU WON'T SEE ME, Lennon-McCartney)
(- 97 -) **BIBLIOGRAPHY / RESOURCES PT. 2**

(- 98 -) 57 YOU'RE GONNA LOSE THAT SOIL (Music: YOU'RE GONNA LOSE THAT GIRL, Lennon-McCartney)
(- 99 -) **BIBLIOGRAPHY / RESOURCES PT. 3**

(- 100 -) **GLOSSARY**

(- 106 -) **INDEX**

(- 112 -) **ORDERING INFORMATION**

FOREWORD

A hippidy sip
from the seed creed
A green scene
inbetween

The Beetless' Gardening Book
Brings the seed creed up to speed
Extols soil toil,
Health wealth
the wiggly worm
and the fertile sperm

while the flood blood makes mud
cover crops stop the flop
of dumb dam denyers
fumbling fleeing fractals
in the harvest time of money.

we chant, rant and cant
to love the gift of life we grow
peace, transcendence and rice
do glow
sowing selection.

benedictions heavy
a ripe harvest grows

to put the clock beneath the ground
entropy crumbles the dust of human vanity.

-- Alan Kapuler, Ph.D.
Research Director, Seeds of Change
January 30, 1997, Corvallis, OR

INTRODUCTION

If poetry, music and gardening have one thing in common (and, of course, they have many things in common), it is that they are inherently participatory. The Beetless know this better than anyone else. Their singular contribution to the late-twentieth-century agri-/horti-/literary/pop cultural scene is contained in the volume you now hold in your hands. You will not fully appreciate it unless you find your own inner poetic voice, which sings quietly without your head even if it's too shy to be heard out loud. And neither will you fully understand or benefit from it unless you become involved in some manner with the production and/or appreciation of your own food.

Inspired by music that they and many of us know and love, the Beetless group formed specifically to write original poems to be read to a backdrop of some of the Beatles' most memorable tunes. As a lark, and as a tribute to Whitman (see p. 3), they sometimes call these poems "songs," and in this book we often indulge their own myth that they are in fact performers.

In the 57 works contained herein they share many of the joys, challenges, and lessons they have derived from their many combined years of organic vegetable gardening in the Pacific Northwest. Sidebars throughout the text list what we know about 43 additional "lost" songs (actually poems, of course) which we hope may one day be recovered.

This is not a regular, stodgy gardening book. It does not pretend to be complete. It acknowledges that gardening is a never-ending process of discovery. Its subversive pretext is that the poetry of everyday experience can tell us as much about gardening as charts, scientific formulas, and know-it-all advice. The Beetless don't know it all. They hope they never do. They hope, however, through these pages, to share some of the most important things they think they do know. If they have succeeded even partially in imparting knowledge, inspiration, useful tips, helpful perspectives, motivation for further exploration, tidbits of wisdom, or a few good belly laughs, they will have deemed themselves successful. If one person starts a garden, learns or tries something new, or is caused to wax poetic (perhaps with modulation of pitch) by these pages, the Beetless mission will be accomplished.

The editor's comments next to each lyric text seek to clarify potentially obscure references and illuminate the context from which the work arose. We trust these annotations will not be considered too intrusive. In addition, a bibliography/resource list (pp. 93, 97, 99), glossary (pp. 100-105), and index (pp. 106-112) will aid studious Beetless fans in deciphering what their idols are so concerned with, and will facilitate self-education about these most vital subjects. (They can then test their new knowledge through the two specially-designed quizzes, on pp. 63 and 67.) A cross-referenced album list on p. 59 will tell you which albums contain the "background songs" for these poems.

A Final Reminder: **Throughout this book, the use of the word "song" is strictly metaphorical and satirical. In reality, the Beetless couldn't hold a tune if their lives depended on it. This hasn't stopped them from creating gardens and enjoying this book. It shouldn't stop you either.**

THE BEETLESS BOOTLEG -- GREAT LOST SONGS OF THE BEETLESS

Jam, Pear, Joychoi and Rutabaga have been prolific lyricists and inexhaustible performers for years now. One of the great tragedies of the modern era is that in general they have held themselves to much higher standards than we have. As a result many of their works have never been recorded (even informally) or written down, and are no longer included in their stage shows. A veritable canon of titles has been lost, at least for the time being. Special sidebars throughout the text include what information we can gather about these "Lost Songs of the Beetless." We eagerly await correspondence from anyone who is able to supply lyrics for these lost Beetless titles.

1
ACROSS THE SEED BEDS FIRST

(Music: ACROSS THE UNIVERSE, Lennon-McCartney)

Cats are prowling out around the corner of my windowbox
They stalk along the fence, look back
To see if I am watching

Cats meander through the open cracks within my garden gate
A strange fear is possessing me

Fie, you prowling felines ... git home
Why you wanna change my world?
Why you wanna change my world?
Why you wanna change my world?
Why you wanna change my world?

Cats approach the garden beds I worked so hard in yesterday
I curse because I know they'll walk
Across the seed beds first

Cats are treating my fresh-planted seed beds as a litter box
They scuff young plants to nothingness
Unsprouted seeds fare worse

Fie, you no-good felines ... git home
Why're you scratching up my world?
Why're you scratching up my world?
Why're you scratching up my world?
Why're you scratching up my world?

Carefully planted furrows vanish like we never put them there
Distressing and incensing me

Clumps of soil land in the path, a smell of kitty lingers there
It stinks that I can't garden when
I plant the seed beds first

Fie, you wretched felines ... go home
Why're you messing up my world?
Why're you messing up my world?
Why're you messing up my world?
Why're you messing up my world?

Fie, you cursed felines
Fie, you prowling felines
Fie, you no-good felines
Fie, you wretched felines
Fie, you stinky felines
Fie, you cursed felines ... *(repeat as above and fade)*

> *Comments:* Unlike the Beatles, for whom THREE COOL CATS was an early stage favorite, the Beetless express a jaded and rather pathetic attitude toward cats in their work. A good friend and neighbor agrees, believing that cats have no place in the middle of a forest, and rejoicing in the bird life that surrounds her cat-less cabin. On the other hand, the Beetless' herbalist, living nearer to town, loves cats. Even the Beetless would probably agree that cats do reduce rodent populations in food storage areas.

> The Beetless Bootleg: Great Lost Songs of the Beetless Pt. 1
> 58 **AND I SLUG HUNT** (Music: AND I LOVE HER, Lennon-McCartney)
>
> A soulful exploration of a subject handled more upbeatly in HERE COME THE SLUGS. Lyrics lost.
>
> 59 **AND YOUR BEES DON'T STING** (Music: AND YOUR BIRD CAN SING, Lennon-McCartney)
>
> Once the Beetless learn more about beekeeping they may resurrect this one.

2
ALL YOUR SEEDS ARE LOVE

(Music: ALL YOU NEED IS LOVE, Lennon-McCartney)

Love, love, love
Love, love, love
Love, love, love

There's some that you can pick into a cup
Some that you can thresh out on a tarp
Some that you can soak a while
Then rinse clean of debris
It's easy

There's some that are tinier than dust
Some that would make your pockets bust
All different shapes and colors
It's biodiversity
And it's easy

All your seeds are love
All your seeds are love
All your seeds are love, love
Love's in all your seeds

Love, love, love
Love, love, love
Love, love, love

All your seeds are love
All your seeds are love
All your seeds are love, love
Love's in all your seeds

Comments: If mere gardening is akin to infatuation, seed-saving is love, the Beetless seem to be saying in this charming number. Recommended reading: *Seed to Seed* by Suzanne Ashworth.

There's some that need burying deep down
Some that will sprout right on the ground
Some that need freezes
Some that need a tropical breeze
It's easy

Some will disappear if they're not saved
Some of our heritage erased
There's past and future pulsing in
These seeds we hold today
It's easy

All your seeds are love
All your seeds are love
All your seeds are love, love
Love's in all your seeds

All your seeds are love (for the children now)
All your seeds are love (and their children)
All your seeds are love, love
Love's in all your seeds

Love's in all your seeds *(24x)*

The Beetless Bootleg: Great Lost Songs of the Beetless Pt. 2
60 BACK IN THE US OF CARS (Music: BACK IN THE USSR, Lennon-McCartney)

Pear scrapped this once he realized how car-dependent he was.

61 THE BALLAD OF WES AND WENDELL (Music: THE BALLAD OF JOHN AND YOKO, Lennon-McCartney)

Like Wes Jackson (see PERMACULTURE GARDEN), author Wendell Berry (*The Unsettling of America*, *The Gift of Good Land*, *What Are People For?*, *Farming: A Hand Book*, and many other titles) is a Beetless hero.

3
BUG ME DO

(Music: LOVE ME DO, Lennon-McCartney)

Bug, bug me do
You know I love you
You'll pollinate too
So please ... bug me do
Whoa-ho bug me do

Bug, bug me do
I'll plant flowers for you
My fruit will come true
So please ... bug me do
Whoa-ho bug me do

Bugs that eat bad bugs
Are bugs that I like too
Bugs don't bother our plants
When we garden in the ways we should do

Bug, bug me do
You'll be my insect zoo
The birds will like it too
So please ... bug me do
Whoa-ho bug me do

Bug, bug me do
I'll always be true
If they spray here I'll sue
So please ... bug me do
Whoa-ho bug me do

Yes, bug me do
Whoa-ho bug me do
Yes, bug me do

Comments: Dating from their early period, this poem reflects the youthful enthusiasm for life that often accompanies discovery of organic vegetable gardening. Market-driven older farmers who have encountered insect problems in unnatural monoculture plantings may grind their teeth at this song, but the Beetless show their own brand of worldly realism when they threaten, "If they spray here I'll sue."

4
CARRY THAT CRATE

(Music: CARRY THAT WEIGHT, Lennon-McCartney)

Boy, you're gonna carry that crate
Carry that crate a long time
Boy, you're gonna carry that crate
Carry that crate a long time

The tire is flat on the wheelbarrow
Trish left her pickup at the service station
The garden cart is on a short vacation
Gabe's in town

Boy, you're gonna carry that crate
Carry that crate a long time
Boy, you're gonna carry that crate
Carry that crate a long time

> *Comments:* Manual labor has a dignity in and of itself, the Beetless imply, at the same time that labor-saving tools may just as frequently be appropriate.

> The Beetless Bootleg: Great Lost Songs of the Beetless Pt. 3
> **62 BEING FOR THE BENEFIT OF ALAN CHADWICK!** (Music: BEING FOR THE BENEFIT OF MR. KITE!, Lennon-McCartney)
>
> Alan Chadwick brought the Biodynamic/French Intensive method of gardening to the United States, transforming a blackberry thicket into a beautiful biointensive garden on a steep hillside at the entrance to the University of California at Santa Cruz main campus. An agroecology apprenticeship program continues his work there. John Jeavons is his most well-known popularizer. Jam patched this one together from an apprenticeship brochure he found in the trash. Lyrics lost.

5
CHICO, YOU'RE A DITCH MAN

(Music: BABY, YOU'RE A RICH MAN, Lennon-McCartney)

How does it feel to be
Loving your land and your people?
How long have you been living there?
Most of your life, I'm told
What have you learned while living there?
Wisdom both true and old

How does it feel to be
Caring for land and for people?
How do you feed your family there?
Garden and fish the sea
How do your plants get water there
In your desert village by the sea?

Chico, you're a ditch man
Chico, you're a ditch man
Chico, you're a *jardinero*

Your garden's laid so carefully
I watch the water flow
Right on the level
And you hold your shovel

Chico, you're a ditch man
Chico, you're a ditch man
Chico, you're a *jardinero*

How does it feel to be
Gardening in such aridity?
Where do you plant all your plants?
Near the top of each ditchside
How wide a ridge do you make?
The ridge and the ditch are equally wide (a foot-and-a-half or so) *

Comments: This one dates from a Beetless trip to a small fishing/farming village on the Sea of Cortez, in Baja California Sur. The name of the village has not been divulged. **Chico** is reportedly the true nickname of a real person. The **Spanish words** tell us that Chico is a **gardener**, a good "**boss**," and a good **teacher**, who believes that agricultural chemicals are **bad for the health**. For more cross-cultural agricultural perspectives, see Michael Ableman's *From the Good Earth: A Celebration of Growing Food Around the World*.

* The Beetless add an explanatory background comment.

Chico, you're a ditch man
Chico, you're a ditch man
Chico, you're *un buen patrón*

I'm working here so happily
Knowing just what level
You are working on
You're helping everyone

Chico, you're a ditch man
Chico, you're a ditch man
Chico, you're *un buen patrón*

Vegetables of every kind
Fruit trees, flowers, herbs are everywhere
What do you think of chemicals?
Malos por la salud
You teach me Spanish while we work
It seems to come so naturally for you

Chico, you're a ditch man
Chico, you're a ditch man
Chico, you're *un buen maestro*

You love your land and people
I wish every son of earth
Could be more like you
Love life as you do

Chico, you're a ditch man
Chico, you're a ditch man
Chico, you're *un buen maestro*

Oh, Chico, you're a ditch man
Chico, you're a ditch man ... *(repeat and fade)*

The Beetless Bootleg: Great Lost Songs of the Beetless Pt. 4

63 BLACKBERRY THICKETS FOREVER (Music: STRAWBERRY FIELDS FOREVER, Lennon-McCartney)

Another tribute to Alan Chadwick, this song asked the question "What if ... ?" (In this case, what if Alan Chadwick had been thrown off campus when he first started ruffling administrators' feathers?)

64 BLUE-GRAY HAY (Music: BLUE JAY WAY, Harrison)

Not much is known.

65 CALLUSY, BLISTERY, SORE (Music: MAGICAL MYSTERY TOUR, Lennon-McCartney)

An uncharacteristically whiny Beetless number, this was quickly deep-sixed.

6
DO YOU WANT TO KNOW THE SEED DEPTH?

(Music: DO YOU WANT TO KNOW A SECRET, Lennon-McCartney)

You'll never know how much soil is above you
But seeds are different, they really care

Listen
Do you want to know the seed depth?
Do you promise you will tell?
Whoa -- closer
Let me whisper in your ear
Say the words you long to hear
There's a general rule -- ooo

Listen (doo-dah-doo)
If you want to know the seed depth (doo-dah-doo)
It depends on lots of things (doo-dah-doo)
Whoa -- closer (doo-dah-doo)
You've a little latitude (doo-dah-doo)
If you want your seeds to grow
But here's the general rule -- ooo

Comments: A surprising reference to mortality starts off this poem, reminding us of the endless cycles of death, decay, regeneration, growth, and decline which inform our gardens and our lives. Otherwise this is standard Beetless fare.

Multiply seed diameter by three or two
Plant at that depth, that should usually do

In dry lands (doo-dah-doo)
You may need to plant them deeper (doo-dah-doo)
In swamps you'll want to plant them shallow (doo-dah-doo)
Whoa -- also (doo-dah-doo)
There are often special cases (doo-dah-doo)
Some smaller seeds need to see light
Seed packets usually have it right -- more or less so -- ooo

7
EARTHWORM

(Music: BLACKBIRD, Lennon-McCartney)

Earthworms working in your garden soil
Contribute to a rich ecology
A harmony
Farming microorganisms too small for our eyes

Earthworms working in your garden soil
Keep all things in balance perfectly
It's home you see
Beneficial microbe populations stay healthy

Earthworms are wise
Earthworms are wise
Wiser by far than you or I

Earthworms are wise
Earthworms are wise
Wiser by far than you or I

Earthworms working in your garden soil
Aerate and enhance fertility
Make it easy
For plant roots to go down and find the sustenance they need
For plant roots to go down and find the sustenance they need
For plant roots to go down and find the sustenance they need

Comments: The Beetless have a knack for summarizing the contents of lengthy scientific treatises in just a few lines, without substantial loss of material. This poem exemplifies this knack, though the Beetless themselves urge their fans to read the books and have the experiences they sing about. "This is just a ditty," Pear has cautioned, "a starting place." We think he's being modest. Their Indian friend Uday Bhawalker helped start them on the "earthworm path." When circumstances allow for it, vermiculture with earthworms, directly in the garden soil, is thought to be superior in many ways to above-ground manure-worm vermiculture in bins. The internationally-distributed *Worm Digest*, published by Beetless friends, discusses the latest developments in both techniques.

FIXING A TOOL

(Music: FIXING A HOLE, Lennon-McCartney)

I'm fixing a tool
And it's raining again
This wasn't broken yesterday
I don't think so

I'm filling the cracks
That run through my life
And keep my mind a-wandering
Where it will go

And it doesn't really matter if I was a suburbanite
If I was an urbanite
Where I was born
There are many people drifting here
Seeking home and wondering
Are their lives now rich or poor?

I'm speaking of doom
And of better lifeways
But still inside I'm wondering
Where it will go

And it doesn't really matter where I was last year
Or if I'm filled with fear
If I'm alone
There are more questions than answers here
Broken hearts, and many tears
Try just looking past your door

Comments (FIXING A TOOL): The Beetless are mum on the meaning of this one.

Comments (GOOD DAY SUNCHOKES): **Spuds** are potatoes. Ninety percent of the earth's vegetable life forms reputedly evolved in a narrow belt of land close to the equator, in regions that are now known as Vavilov Centers. The Beetless' tribute to **sunchokes** (also called Jerusalem artichokes, "dieter's potatoes," and other inaccurate names) reflects upon this situation, which, despite the cheery melody, bears two more somber undersides. First, as the Beetless point out, we have a diminished sense of place because most of our crop varieties have been imported, and we are ignorant of native foodstuffs. Second, perhaps more ominously, something our four lads (fresh from the controversy surrounding MIGUEL) apparently deemed too "heavy" for this song:
(continued in box next page)

I'm fixing a tool
And it's raining again
I hear earth and
 people calling me
Where I will go
Where I will go
I'm fixing a tool
And it's raining again
A voice inside is
 calling me
Where I will go
Where I will go

> ... urban settlement, deforestation, and importation of hybrid seed varieties are rapidly wiping out ancient natural varieties and entire ecosystems within these Vavilov Centers. We may indeed be singing GOOD DAY SUNCHOKES before too long, if the seedstocks that form the genetic reservoirs for our cultivated varieties continue to disappear at their
> *(continued below)*

9
GOOD DAY SUNCHOKES

(Music: GOOD DAY SUNSHINE, Lennon-McCartney)

Good day sunchokes, good day sunchokes, good day sunchokes

I like to learn where crops are native to
North America has just a few
Sunflowers and berries, cran- and blue-
And excluding wild vegetables, one's gotta do

Good day sunchokes, good day sunchokes, good day sunchokes

Tomatoes, beans, corn, spuds and squash
All came up from further south ...

> ...present rate. If biodiversity's gone and a blight hits, sunchokes may be all that we're eating. Luckily, they're quite good.

Good day sunchokes, good day sunchokes, good day sunchokes

Most of our diet comes from afar
Europe, Asia, Africa
Central and South America
We still don't know just where we are

Good day sunchokes, good day sunchokes, good day sunchokes
Good day sunchokes *(repeat and fade)*

10
GOPHER BITES

(Music: HOLD ME TIGHT, Lennon-McCartney)

I feel uptight now ...

Gopher bites
Tell me these are the only ones
And then I might
Know that my garden's not undone

But gopher bites
And bites
And bites
Make me blue
Blue, blue, blue -- ooo

Gopher bites
I see plants tremble violently
Then with great might
They disappear entirely

'Cause gopher bites
And bites
And bites
Make me blue
Blue, blue, blue -- ooo

Oh gopher bites
All through the carrot bed I had grown
They've got the parsley and the broccoli too

It's such a fright it's ...

Gopher bites
Three dozen plants become just one
As if in spite
They're ruining my garden fun

Comments: Another self-explanatory Beetless lyric. Gophers tunnel, and like the taste of roots. "Gopher plant" might possibly repel them if planted in a solid block all the way around one's garden, but in most situations it has proven useless; gophers simply eat everything else. It's only fair to note that, if you don't mind growing food for them, gophers do help break up and cultivate soil, improve drainage, and create freshly-tilled mounds for seeds to sprout in.

When gopher bites
And bites
And bites
Make me blue
Blue, blue, blue -- ooo

Oh gopher bites
All through the cabbage and the kale
They've got the parsnips and potatoes too

It's out of sight it's ...

Gopher bites
I think I'll try a trap or two
And then I might
Have a crack at seeing the season through

'Cause gopher bites
And bites
And bites
Make me blue
Blue, blue, blue -- ooo
Blue -- ooo

The Beetless Bootleg:
Great Lost Songs of
the Beetless Pt. 5

66 COMPOST TOGETHER
(Music: COME TOGETHER, Lennon-McCartney)

Though very difficult to sing, this song did have something going for it that other compost-related Beetless tunes do not: it mentioned the importance of starting each layer by building the edges first, then filling in the center, for better structural integrity. This was not enough to save it.

---

67 CSA DAY (Music: SEXY SADIE, Lennon-McCartney)

The Beetless' one and only attempt thus far to describe the workings of a Community Supported Agriculture project, this portrayed a typical harvest/pickup day. The clumsy cadence of many of the lyrics caused them to retract it, despite the importance of its subject. (See I WANT TO SELL YOU comments.)

68 A DAY IN THE LEAF (Music: A DAY IN THE LIFE, Lennon-McCartney)

Jam and Pear trade thoughts about photosynthesis.

11
GOT TO PICK YOU, NOT USE A KNIFE

(Music: GOT TO GET YOU INTO MY LIFE, Lennon-McCartney)

I was alone, I took a walk
I didn't know what I would find there
Another plant that might be good
As food or medicine -- free wild fare

Ooo, then I got this strange feeling
Ooo, and some voice kept repeating
Harvesting is sacred, not a chore

You didn't run, you didn't hide
You knew I wanted just to hold you
Until I'd looked and knew for sure
That there were many more just like you

Ooo, then I sensed you were near me
Ooo, and I wanted you to hear me
I knew what ol' Tom Ward would surely say

Got to pick you, not use a knife

What can I do, now that I see
I'm with you in a bounteous stand here
Brothers and sisters all around
They can afford to have you leave here

Ooo, then I suddenly hear you
Ooo, Tom Ward said I should heed you
Asking me to put away my knife

Got to pick you, not use a knife

I got to pick you, not use a knife

Comments:
Tom Ward, an herbalist, wildcrafter, Permaculture instructor, and appropriate-living guru, was one of the Beetless' earliest inspirations and also one of their earliest fans. His book *Greenward, Ho!* explains his preferred method of harvesting: gripping the desired plant part firmly between thumb and forefinger, and using the action of the third finger to remove it from the parent plant.

I was alone with your insides
I felt the tissues' vital force there
It didn't want a metal cut
Instead it wanted loving hand-tear

What's left heals more quickly
What's harvested's more healthy
Hands-on helps us pray ...

The Beetless Bootleg: Great Lost Songs of the Beetless Pt. 6

69 **DEAR RODENTS** (Music: DEAR PRUDENCE, Lennon-McCartney)

The Beetless stopped singing this when GOPHER BITES proved more of a crowd-pleaser.

70 **DON'T LET ME DROWN** (Music: DON'T LET ME DOWN, Lennon-McCartney)

Fans protested that this "instructional" watering song was overly didactic and insulting.

71 **DON'T STEP ON ME** (Music: DON'T BOTHER ME, Lennon-McCartney)

Another case of rubbing fans the wrong way; the words of warning in SHE SAID RAISED BED, the Beetless decided, would have to suffice.

72 **DRIVE MY TRACTOR** (Music: DRIVE MY CAR, Lennon-McCartney)

The Beetless' romance with tractors was short-lived, as was this song. They could never get the timing right.

12
GRASSMAN

(Music: TAXMAN, Harrison)

Let me tell you how it will be
Golf courses far as eyes can see
'Cause I'm the Grassman
Yeah, I'm the Grassman

Green lawns in each suburban yard
Green pastures where we grow our lard
'Cause I'm the Grassman
Yeah, I'm the Grassman

Though you'd like it wild, I want it neat
Though you'd like it diverse, I want
    everything discreet
Though you'd like some native species,
    I want some meat
As for homegrown food, I don't want
    you to eat

Grassman

'Cause I'm the Grassman
Yeah, I'm the Grassman

Comments: A Beetless foray into politics and lifestyle issues, which they see as intrinsically related to their gardening lives. Much of the world's grass seed is grown in Oregon's Willamette Valley, the Beetless' home turf, where fields are regularly burned as a "sanitary" measure, releasing smoke that may be heavily laden with dioxins. Typically, though conveying a serious message, the Beetless here take a somewhat lighthearted, nonbombastic approach.

Don't ask me why I burn my seedfields (ha ha, smoke emissions)
If you don't want me to burn some more (ha ha, scorched earth)
'Cause I'm the Grassman
Yeah, I'm the Grassman

Now my response if you wonder why (Grassman)
There's laws against lawns that grow too high (Grassman)
Is I'm the Grassman
I'm not the Meadowman, no

And you're mowing for no one but me (Grassman)

13
GREENS THAT ARE MUSTARDS

(Music: MEAN MR. MUSTARD, Lennon-McCartney)

Greens that are mustards
Pack quite a punch
Have them for lunch
Breakfast or dinner

Some look like they're coated with wax
Why is that so? you may ask
It's to shed saltspray, and make freshwater last
They're descended from sea cabbage
Sea cabbage

Broccoli leaves, collards
Kale, cress, bok choy
Arugula -- greens
Just don't get better

Feed 'em lime, oak leaves, egg shells and bones
Limestone seacliffs once were their home
They're full of minerals, not calcium alone
And rich in vitamins
Vitamins

Comments: The names "**mustards**," "brassicas," "crucifers," and "cole crops" are used interchangeably for members of the cabbage family, Brassicaceae. **Lime** is commonly used to reduce soil acidity (raise pH) -- something also accomplished by the addition of wood ash and/or compost. Despite their tannic acid content, **oak leaves** contain a significant amount of calcium (as do lime, **egg shells**, and **bones**), which mustards appreciate. Like three-year-olds, the Beetless are forever asking not only "What?," but "Why?," a trait that often comes in handy to a gardener when considering the needs of various vegetable crops.

14
A HARD CLAY SOIL

(Music: A HARD DAY'S NIGHT, Lennon-McCartney)

I've got a hard, clay soil
And I've been working like a dog
To add humus so that when it rains
I've got a garden, not a bog
But when the dry season comes
Instead of fertile, rich crumbs
It's still like a concrete log

You know I work all day
Digging ditches, adding mulch
I've tried forking, and been known to pray
For soil imported from Green Gulch
But when I get home at night
I know the garden's alright
As our veggie bin starts to bulge

When I'm home everything seems to be right
When I'm home -- but then I'm dreaming of bentonite, -nite, yeah

There are more nutrients in heavy clay
Than in pure sand, which drains too fast
But if I could really have my way
I'd like a loam that's made to last
I'd leave these harsh hillsides for
The fertile valley floor
A garden there would be a blast
Ow!

I'd leave these harsh hillsides for
The fertile valley floor
A garden there would be a blast

Comments: **Humus** is a brown or black organic substance resulting from the decay of vegetable or animal matter. **Crumbs** are aggregates of soil particles -- the bigger the better, for water and air infiltration. **Mulch** refers to a material applied to the surface of the soil, in this case to provide nutrients and organic matter. (It can also prevent evaporation of moisture, reduce weeds, prevent soil erosion, or moderate, raise, or reduce soil temperature.) **Loam** is a benevolent mixture of sand (large particles of disintegrated rock, often silicate), clay (fine particles), silt (intermediate-size particles), and organic matter. **Green Gulch** is a Zen Meditation Center with enviable garden soil. **Bentonite** is a type of clay used to line ponds, dams, and the "homesteader's bathtub."

When I'm home everything seems to be right
When I'm home -- but then I'm dreaming of bentonite, -nite, yeah

I've got a hard, clay soil
And I'll be working it 'til I rot
'Cause in pleasure and in toil
What you've got is what you've got
So at the end of the day
I'll still be feeling ok
'Cause I've been doing what I ought

I've been doing what I ought
I've been doing what I ought

Further Comments: It's extraordinarily important to understand that the Beetless are a product of their time and their place. The time: an interlude between ice ages, though "hothouse earth" is a wildcard. The place: a hard clay soil. Like all homes, like life itself, this soil inspires a love-hate relationship that the Beetless have been trying for a long time to express eloquently.

The Beetless Bootleg: Great Lost Songs of the Beetless Pt. 7

73 FOR NO SUN (Music: FOR NO ONE, Lennon-McCartney)

A ponderous exploration of all the different reasons a plant may have withered and died. After considering lack of nutrients, lack of water, insect attack, bird attack, gopher attack, slug attack, rabbit attack, deer attack, symphylan attack, disease, allelopathy, unfavorable weather, genetic weakness, improper pH, and ultraviolet radiation, Pear decides it must have been for lack of sun.

74 GET STACKED (Music: GET BACK, Lennon-McCartney)

A rocking Permaculture song about stacking functions and encouraging synergism. (See PERMACULTURE GARDEN.) Pear says he accidentally used the written lyrics as rabbit bedding, and can't remember them.

HERE COME THE SLUGS

(Music: HERE COMES THE SUN, Harrison)

Here come the slugs (do-n-do-do)
Here come the slugs
'n' I say, what a fright

Little darling, it's been a long wet lonely winter
Little darling, I think that spring will soon be here

Here come the slugs (do-n-do-do)
Here come the slugs
'n' I say, my flashlight

Little darling, the seedlings entering slug faces
Little darling, I'm seeing slug slime everywhere

Here come the slugs
Here come the slugs
'n' I say, slug bucket

Slugs, slugs, slugs, here they come
Slugs, slugs, slugs, here they come
Slugs, slugs, slugs, here they come
Slugs, slugs, slugs, here they come
Slugs, slugs, slugs, here they come

Little darling, I value every living being
Little darling, but I am chopping them in two

Comments: Slug-hunting is often performed most effectively at night, hence the reference to "my flashlight." Though almost universally despised among Pacific Northwest gardeners, slugs have their charms. Here they have the Beetless singing a surprisingly hopeful, cheery tune, whose message seems to transcend the occasional "downer" lyric. This is the closest we may ever get to a human-sung slug love song. David George Gordon's *Field Guide to the Slug* is an essential reference for anyone living in slug country. For a more personal perspective read "A Slug-hunter's Awakening," which brought temporary notoriety to its author when first published in newsletter form (it now appears in *The Lost Valley Book of Ecological Cooking and Living*).

Here come the slugs (do-n-do-do)
Here come the slugs
'n' I say, my spade please

Here come the slugs (do-n-do-do)
Here come the slugs
(and they stay) 'til summer
'Til summer

The Beetless Bootleg: Great Lost Songs of the Beetless Pt. 8
75 **GLASS GREENHOUSE** (Music: GLASS ONION, Lennon-McCartney)

Discussed the importance of proper orientation, adequate ventilation, thermal mass, and appropriate glazing and roof angles. The engineers in the crowd loved it, but no one else could get into it.

76 **HAPPINESS IS THE WARM SUN** (Music: HAPPINESS IS A WARM GUN, Lennon-McCartney)

The title says it all. It's a shame this was lost.

77 **HEY BULLFROG** (Music: HEY BULLDOG, Lennon-McCartney)

The Beetless address the topic of natives vs. exotics. A nonnative invader on the Beetless' home turf, bullfrogs eat the native tree frogs. Parallel events in human history are disturbingly numerous.

16
I SAW HERBS STANDING THERE

(Music: I SAW HER STANDING THERE, Lennon-McCartney)

Well, the garden was so green
You know what I mean
And the way it smelled was way beyond compare
So how could I walk any further
When I saw herbs standing there?

The flowers and the bees
The birds in the trees
The sunshine and the fresh September air
So how could I walk any further
When I saw herbs standing there?

Well my secaturs went snip
And I bit my lip
I had cut down an old grape vine ...

So I ran to the woods
Pursued by all these shoulds
But I came upon a meadow bright and fair
And how could I run any further
When I saw herbs standing there?

> **Comments:**
> **Secaturs** are an expensive cross between scissors and pruning shears. The whimsical nature of this lyric belies its deeper meanings.

Well my heart went boom
When I realized that soon
Civilization might fade away ...

But in the interlude
For medicine or food
Wildcrafted herbs might really, really pay

So how could I take over my father's drugstore -- ooo
When I saw herbs standing there?
Whoa since I saw herbs standing there
Yeah since I saw herbs standing there

I TILL

(Music: I WILL, Lennon-McCartney)

God knows how much I've tilled you
God knows I'm tilling still
It can keep me pretty busy
'Cause I'm wanting to
I till

Chop earthworms into pieces
Turn colloids into dust
Ruin the structure, collapse the tunnels
'Cause I'm 'xpected to
I till

Bring all the weed seeds to the surface
Give them a fresh new start
Upset the natural ecosystem
Ruin a work of art

*Kill microbes, snakes, and critters
Snuff crops, but spread quackgrass
Invert layers, induce runoff
'Cause I'm feeling blue, I till

*Bring all the weed seeds to the surface
Give them a fresh new start
Upset the natural ecosystem
Ruin a work of art

And when at last I've killed you
The ground completely bare
Compacted beyond recognition
By my trusty old ignition
I will still be fond of your condition
Park my tractor there, I will
I will

Comments: * The Beetless add an extra verse and extra bridge to the Beatles' original tune. **Colloids** are substances composed of many tiny particles suspended in a gel-like mass, with a lot of surface area in proportion to their weight; they are important in soils both chemically and structurally. (For further information about colloids, crumbs, aggregates, and other difficult soil terms, consult *The Soul of Soil* by Grace Gershuny and Joseph Smillie.) **Soil microorganisms** live at specific soil depths; when layers are disturbed or inverted, those microbes too far from their "home depth" die.
    Masters of sincerity and good intentions, the Beetless are, however, not above the occasional satire.

18
I WANNA FREEZE AND CAN

(Music: I WANNA BE YOUR MAN, Lennon-McCartney)

I wanna eat well this winter, baby
I wanna freeze and can
I wanna eat well this winter, baby
I wanna freeze and can

I'll eat right out of the garden, baby
Every time I can
But some crops just don't last there, baby
I wanna freeze and can

I wanna freeze and can
I wanna freeze and can
I wanna freeze and can
I wanna freeze and can

I also wanna sun-dry, baby
And store stuff in the house
I'll use my root cellar for root crops, baby
And seal it against the Mouse

I wanna eat well this winter, baby
In every way I can
I'll dry, store, cellar, and harvest fresh, baby
And I wanna freeze and can

I wanna freeze and can
I wanna freeze and can
I wanna freeze and can
I wanna freeze and can

I need no supermarkets, baby
I don't want that food they sell
It's dead or it's laced with chemicals, baby
But in my garden I can grow food well

Comments: A lusty ode to food preservation, this has become a cult classic in pantries, freezers, and (to a lesser extent) root cellars all over the Beetless' "home territory." Consulting *Putting Food By* or some similar reliable reference is highly recommended, especially when canning.

I've got no use for fast food, baby
I know it's just a sham
Time is love in the garden, baby
I wanna freeze and can

I wanna freeze and can
I wanna freeze and can
I wanna freeze and can
I wanna freeze and can

I wanna freeze and can *(repeat and fade)*

The Beetless Bootleg: Great Lost Songs of the Beetless Pt. 9
78 **HOE SNAP PEAS, HOE FAVAS** (Music: OB-LA-DI, OB-LA-DA, Lennon-McCartney)

Snap peas and fava beans can both be grown overwinter in the Pacific Northwest -- a fact that this song celebrated. Because success with favas proved significantly easier than success with overwintered snap peas, the Beetless withdrew it pending revision.

79 **I AM THE FARMER** (Music: I AM THE WALRUS, Lennon-McCartney)

A strange one about farming and identity.

80 **I DIG A POTATO** (Music: I DIG A PONY, Lennon-McCartney)

The Beetless stopped doing this when they discovered that they could harvest potatoes by hand-picking from under mulch (see PAPERBACK MULCHER).

19
I WANT TO DIG BY HAND

(Music: I WANT TO HOLD YOUR HAND, Lennon-McCartney)

Well I'll tell your something
I hope you'll understand
I don't want no rototiller
I want to dig by hand

I want to dig by hand
I want to dig by hand

Well tractors make me queasy
Their noise I cannot stand
Their fumes, they sure are stinky
I want to dig by hand

I want to dig by hand
I want to dig by hand

And when I touch soil
I feel happy inside
It's such a feeling
That my love for it
I can't hide
I can't hide
I can't hide

The soil stays uncompacted
The critters aren't so scammed
So when it's necessary even to mess
  with it
I want to dig by hand

I want to dig by hand
I want to dig by hand

Comments: **Garden spades** (with rectangular heads) are far superior to pointy-tipped shovels for digging garden beds. **Digging forks** (whose tines are stronger than those on pitchforks and not flat like those on potato forks) are often even better. It's worth looking for long-handled tools, which can reduce back strain. The Beetless love this song, but are careful to whom they sing it. Many farmers who have occasionally employed them have never heard it. This should not diminish the validity of its message, which posits a world in which our convictions and our passions need not bow down before expediency and false economics.

Sometimes a garden fork
Is all you need
It does less damage
And leaves soil
So crumbly
So crumbly
So crumbly

But spades and forks, they keep me happy
I know you understand
I don't want no rototiller
I'll spade and fork by hand

I want to dig by hand
I want to dig by hand
I want to dig by hand

The Beetless Bootleg: Great Lost Songs of the Beetless Pt. 10

81 I SHOULD HAVE SOWN BETTER (Music: I SHOULD HAVE KNOWN BETTER, Lennon-McCartney)

A belabored, self-castigating number about why seeds might not have sprouted as desired: planted too deep, too shallow, too thick, too thin, or from stock that had never matured, was poorly stored, was too old, was genetically inferior, of the wrong variety, of the wrong species, or a bad choice to begin with. Downer lyrics we don't miss.

82 I'M SOW-TIRED (Music: I'M SO TIRED, Lennon-McCartney)

Another uncharacteristically discouraged, discouraging lyric, written before the lads had learned to pace themselves.

20
I WANT TO SELL YOU

(Music: I WANT TO TELL YOU, Harrison)

I want to sell you
I'm tired of giving good food away
But it's weird
I never know what to do at the end of the day

Farmers markets are funny
We overharvest and they underbuy
Pick less next week
We'll be sold out 'fore half the day's gone by

If we all had gardens things would be fine
Our harvesting would be in line
With what we needed

When I first grew you
You looked so happy in your place in the sun
So healthy and fine
Harvesting you just wasn't any fun

But now I'm selling you for cash
To get the money to buy the gas
To pay to get you here

I want to sell you
I don't know what will happen to you
Will you be food
Or will the soup kitchen even recognize you?

Should I compost you?

What should I do?

Comments: The Beetless are all too familiar with the plight of many vegetables and the farmers who steward them in this existence. This song demonstrates their empathy, while shedding light on a regrettable situation and suggesting a more desirable alternative. Surprisingly, they don't mention Community Supported Agriculture, a farmer-consumer partnership in which shareholders typically receive a weekly basket full of various vegetables in exchange for a yearly fee and often some level of participation in the farm. (See CSA DAY, in Lost Songs section).

21
I'M A SHROOMER

(Music: I'M A LOSER, Lennon-McCartney)

I'm a shroomer
I'm a shroomer
I'm in love with mushrooms can't you see

Come every fall, once the rains really start
Sprout fruiting bodies dear to my heart
Bearing spores of fungi that live underground
Bursting through duff without making a sound

I'm a shroomer
In the forest I feel so free
I'm a shroomer
If you try it, I'm sure you'll agree

Here symbiotic relationships abound
Fungi feed roots, and the other way around
The trees give dry-season water and sap
Fungi bring nutrients from all over the map

I'm a shroomer
I'm almost sure of its edibility
I'm a shroomer
Unless it's not what it appears to be

Mycorrhizal fungi keep soil rich and alive
Help trees and microbes alike to survive
Saprophytes break down dead matter instead
And parasites will make live matter dead

I'm a shroomer
I'm surrounded by virility
I'm a shroomer
I'm in love with mushrooms can't you see

Comments: In this song the Beetless carefully avoid suggesting the harvesting of any particular mushroom species. In private conversation they recommend the purchase of a reliable field guide (such as David Arora's *Mushrooms Demystified*, especially good in the Pacific Northwest) and multiple trips to field or forest with an experienced mushroomer before attempting anything on one's own. Their intention here is simply to awaken their listeners to the wonders of the mushroom world.

22
I'M EATING GOOD FOOD

(Music: I'M LOOKING THROUGH YOU, Lennon-McCartney)
(Poem: Copyright © 1997 Larry Dobberstein)

I'm eating good food -- not long ago
I thought I ate well -- what did I know?
My life is different, I'll take a stand
I'm eating good food, I'm a new man

No more fried chicken, no tuna fish
Don't put no bacon on my food dish
Just pass the pasta and broccoli too
I'm eating good food, make mine tofu

Why, tell me why, are we not eating right?
Commercials leave a nasty habit of craving
   junkfood day and night

My blood is moving, healthy and free
I've more endurance and energy
Industrial food sucks, I've learned their game
Let's all eat good food, organic grain

Why, tell me why, are we not eating right?
Commercials leave a nasty habit of craving
   junkfood day and night

My blood is moving, healthy and free
I've more endurance and energy
Industrial food sucks, I've learned their game
I'm eating good food, I'm not the same

I'm eating good food ...
Organic carrots ...
Baby I've changed ... *(etc.; repeat and fade)*

Comments: One of only two Beetless "covers," this was written by EarthSave activist, video artist, and longtime Beetless fan Larry Dobberstein of Eugene, OR, who sent it to the lads on a whim, never thinking they'd perform it. But true to their roots among the "commoners" and their continued rapport with their less famous peers, they added it almost immediately to their repertoire. You too could have your name in the Beetless program credits, if your poetry's good enough.

MEET THE BEETLESS

This is your space to draw the fab four.

Jam Lemon　　　　　*Pear Machete*

Joychoi Heirloom　　　　　*Rutabaga Variety*

23
IT'S ALL GOOD MULCH

(Music: IT'S ALL TOO MUCH, Harrison)

To our Mother ...

It's all good mulch
It's all good mulch

When I look into the sties
Where you kept your piggy
I find such a richness there
It fills me up with glee

It's all good mulch for me to take
Organic matter all around me
Dung and food scraps, there's no waste
It's what I take
It's all good mulch

When I walk the alleyways
Of any town or city
I find such abundance there
It's like a shopping spree

It's all good mulch for me to take
Organic matter all around me
Cardboard, paper, cannery waste
It's what I take
It's all good mulch

When I drive by my neighbor's yard
Or visit the horse stable
I come back for load after load
To stop I am not able

The Beetless Bootleg: Great Lost Songs of the Beetless Pt. 11

83 THE INNER BITE (Music: THE INNER LIGHT, Harrison)

Contemplated the essence of the archetypal homegrown vegetable. Lyrics lost.

84 MARKETS ARE NEAR (Music: MARTHA MY DEAR, Lennon-McCartney)

An early foray into agricultural economics.

85 MELON SAYS PICK ME (Music: ELEANOR RIGBY, Lennon-McCartney)

An exhaustive "instructional" song about when different crops are ready for harvest. Regrettably, nobody came to its only public performance, and the Beetless dropped it from their repertoire.

It's all good mulch for me to take
Organic matter all around me
Leaves, grass clippings, all yard waste
It's what I take
It's all good mulch

It's all good mulch for me to take
Organic matter all around me
Manure and straw and rotten hay
It's what I take
It's all good mulch

It's good mulch
It's good mulch

It is everywhere and it's free for use
It is everywhere and it's free for use

It's good mulch
Alive or dead ...

Good mulch *(50x)*

> *Comments:* It should be noted that leaves, grass clippings, and yard waste are safe to apply as mulch only if they come from land that has not been sprayed with chemicals. One of several Beetless songs about mulch, this one surpasses the others several times over in the number of times the word is used.

The Beetless Bootleg: Great Lost Songs of the Beetless Pt. 12

86 **P.S. I LOVE FOOD** (Music: P.S. I LOVE YOU, Lennon-McCartney)

A catchy number, but all anyone remembers is the refrain.

87 **REDISTRIBUTION** (Music: REVOLUTION, Lennon-McCartney)

Cautiously wading into issues of land distribution, the Beetless just as cautiously retreated, and pulled this song back with them.

24
I'VE GOT A SEEDLING

(Music: I'VE GOT A FEELING, Lennon-McCartney)

I've got a seedling, a seedling that's inside
Oh yeah, oh yeah (that's right)
It's getting big now, it's starting to have pride
Oh no, no -- oh no
Oh no, yeah, yeah!
I've got a seedling, yeah

This seedling tells me, it's tired of being soft
Oh yeah, (yeah) oh yeah
It's tired of shelter, it wants to harden off
Oh no, oh no
Oh no, yeah, yeah!
I've got a seedling, yeah
I've got a seedling

I'll bring it outside of the greenhouse for now
Maybe take it in if the night is kinda cold
Bring it out tomorrow, in a few days back-and-forthing will be through

(Ooo) I've got a seedling that's aching for the ground
Oh yeah, oh yeah (oh yeah)
Its pot's too small now, its roots are curling round
Oh no, oh no (oh no)
Oh no -- no, no!
I'll plant that seedling, yeah (yeah)

Root crops had a fairly hard year
Flowers had a pretty good time
Vinefruits ripened like a sweet dream
On account of all the sunshine
Oh yeah (oh yeah), oh yeah, oh yeah

Leaf crops had a pretty good year
Grains experienced a blowdown
Seedcrops couldn't keep their stalks up (no)
Early plantings nearly all drowned, oh yeah

Root crops had a fairly good year (I've got a seedling)
Flowers had a pretty hard time (a seedling I can't hide, oh no)
Vinefruits molded like a bad dream (oh no)
On account of lack of sunshine

Grain crops had a pretty good year (I've got a seedling)
Leaves got weedy and were hoed down (that's reaching for the sky, oh yeah)
Seedcrops nearly kept their stalks up (oh yeah yeah yeah)
Early plantings had a rebound, oh yeah

I've got a seedling (oh yeah)
I've got a seedling (oh yeah)
I've got a seedling, yeah, yeah, yeah, yeah

Comments: Personal gardening poems are a Beetless trademark. Here the plant's dilemna becomes the gardener's dilemna, the plant's desire inseparable from the gardener's desire to satisfy it. We sense that the plant will repay the gardener's solicitude many times over. Yet we are reminded that, as in life, nothing is predictable, and results are always different.

The Beetless Bootleg: Great Lost Songs of the Beetless Pt. 13
88 ROLL OVER J. LIEBIG (Music: ROLL OVER BEETHOVEN, Chuck Berry)

Baron Justus von Liebig, the father of reductionist soil chemistry, is told what to do with his theories.

I'VE JUST SEEN A FROST

(Music: I'VE JUST SEEN A FACE, Lennon-McCartney)

I've just seen a frost
I can't forget the plants I've lost
Because I didn't keep them decently
Protected -- I mean essentially
They died
Died, died, died, die-die-died

Had it been perpetual day
They would have looked the other way
At 35 F they wouldn't have frozen
But those clear night skies they caught 'em dozin'
They died
Died, died, died, die-die-died

Fallin', temperature's fallin'
And I feel maudlin
Remembering when

American crops like tomatoes
Peppers, eggplants, potatoes
Corn and beans, and basil too
Live or die depending what you do
At night
Night, night, night, nigh-nigh-night

Fallin', temperature's fallin'
And I feel maudlin
Remembering when

Fallin', temperature's fallin'
And I feel maudlin
Remembering when

Comments: The "**American**" **crops** referred to (basil is not a part of this list) come from Central or South America. **Reemay** is the brand name of a spun polyester fiber which can protect against light frosts. **Carrots** survive mild but not heavy freezes. Radiation frosts -- frosts which occur under clear night skies at air temperatures above freezing -- are legendary among gardeners, and are thought to occur most frequently around the time of a full moon.

From 32 to 38
They can die of cold or can look just great
If covered with Reemay or a sheet
Or sprinkled overhead, they may still taste sweet
The next day
Day, day, day, day-day-day

Sullen, yes I'm sullen
Cell walls are explodin'
With the cold

Carrots soon need diggin'
Or we'll be eatin'
Mush and mold

Fallin', temperature's fallin'
And I feel maudlin
Remembering when

The Beetless Bootleg: Great Lost Songs of the Beetless Pt. 14

89 **THE ROOT CELLAR'S COOL -- USE IT** (Music: ROCK AND ROLL MUSIC, Chuck Berry)

Though understandably dropped because no one could sing the verses, this did highlight an important technique that I WANNA FREEZE AND CAN mentions only in passing. Only the title remains.

90 **SAVOY CABBAGE** (Music: SAVOY TRUFFLE, Harrison)

An unusual tribute to a single vegetable, this was quite popular for a while until fans said they'd had enough of it.

26
I'VE JUST SEEN A PLACE

(Music: I'VE JUST SEEN A FACE, Lennon-McCartney)

I've just seen a place
I can't forget, I think there's space
To stick another little seedling there
I didn't realize that there were quite
So many
Mmm, mmm, mmm -- mmm

Had it been another bed
I think I'd probably have said
We can't squeeze any more starts in
But as it is these plants are all
Companions
La da da, da n da

Companions
Yes, companions
Carrots and onions
Corn and beans

I'd never known complexity
But gardening has let me see
How elements all intertwine
In ecosystems
Symbiotically
Dee dee dee, dee dee dee

Companions
Yes, companions
Cabbage and peppermint
Garlic and beets

The Beetless Bootleg: Great Lost Songs of the Beetless Pt. 15

91 **SHE'S KNOWING HOME** (Music: SHE'S LEAVING HOME, Lennon-McCartney)

A bioregional anthem to the joys of home gardening. We'd love to dig this one out again.

92 **SLOPE DOWN** (Music: SLOW DOWN, Larry Williams)

An intriguing but clumsy exploration of different factors in garden siting: not only slope but sun angle, shading, soil conditions, existing vegetation, historical use, drainage, proximity to buildings, integration with the landscape, and the overall "feel" of the site. A great idea but poorly executed and with an inappropriate title, it unceremoniously disappeared from the Beetless' performances.

Companions
Yes, companions
Spinach and strawberries
Turnips and peas

Companions complement each other
In nutrient and water requirements
Growth habits and demands for light
Attract good bugs and give bad ones
A fright
La da da, da da da

Companions
Yes, companions
Spuds and marigolds
Kale and camomile

Companions
Yes, companions
Lettuce and cucumbers
Asparagus and parsley

* Companions discourage diseases
Promote soil life and keep down weeds
But life's not known by disection
Our understanding's only just
Begun
Mmm, mmm, mmm, da n da

One final note: antagonists
Don't help, but hinder one another
But that's another story I
Don't want to sing, it's not nearly so
   much
Fun
Nigh-nigh-nigh, la n da

(continued next page)

> ***Comments:*** * All verses from "Companions discourage diseases" to the end are "extras," added on by the Beetless to the Beatles' original tune.
>
> Forever incurable romantics, the Beetless can't resist drawing a comparison between plant compatibility and romantic love in the closing lines of this song. In other ways, both spirit and content undoubtedly owe a large debt to biointensive gardening guru John Jeavons, founder of Ecology Action and author of *How to Grow More Vegetables ... than you ever thought possible on less land than you can imagine*, one of the Beetless' dog-eared mainstays.

Antagonists
Oh, antagonists
Peas and onions
Carrots and dill

Antagonists
Oh, antagonists
Cabbage and strawberries
Tomatoes and fennel

But I've just seen a place
I feel there's space to put a seedling there
If it adds to the harmony
If so, I'll want the world to see
This bed
Mmm, mmm, mmm, la da da

Companions
Yes, companions
Nasturtiums and radishes
Tomatoes and mints

Oh, companions
Yes, companions
Long-time lovers
Best friends

The Beetless Bootleg:
Great Lost Songs of the
Beetless Pt. 16

93 **THE TOOL ON THE HILL** (Music: THE FOOL ON THE HILL, Lennon-McCartney)

The Beetless are working on a new song about tool care and the importance of putting away tools at night. This old one did more to offend garden helpers than to enlighten them.

94 **TURDS OF LOVE** (Music: WORDS OF LOVE, Buddy Holly)

When THE TURD proved more popular and easier to sing than TURDS OF LOVE, the Beetless gladly made the switch. Few regret it.

---

95 **WHEN I'M SICK AND SORE** (Music: WHEN I'M SIXTY-FOUR, Lennon-McCartney)

A whiny number along the lines of CALLUSY, BLISTERY, SORE, this died a welcome death at about the same time.

27
THE LONG ERODED PATH

(Music: THE LONG AND WINDING ROAD, Lennon-McCartney)

The long, eroded path
That leads from your door
May never disappear
I've seen erosion there before
The water flows through bootprints there
Drainage is really poor

I tried sowing clover seeds
After raking the surface fine
I even watered it
And marked it off with lime
But it's still eroding there
Gets wiped out every time

Many times I've seen that path
And many times I've tried
To keep others from walking there
Until that clover's high

Peg slipped and hurt her back
On that long, eroded path
Mike took a nosedive there
Rushing to a class
He said he'd walked with care
But it went downhill real fast

And still I'm taken aback
By that long, eroded path
Nothing will establish there
Once footprints come to pass
The soil's almost always bare
It can't even grow crabgrass

Comments:
Perennial **clovers** fix atmospheric nitrogen in the soil (as most legumes do) while providing cover and compostable greens when sown in paths. **Crabgrass** is a tenacious perennial rhizomatous grass which spreads by means of underground runners.
   Always drawing lessons from adversity, the Beetless have developed over the course of many years the serenity to accept the things they cannot change, the courage to change the things they can, and the wisdom to know the difference.

28
LOOSELY FIRM THE EDGES OF SEEDFLATS

(Music: LUCY IN THE SKY WITH DIAMONDS,
Lennon-McCartney)

Picture yourself with a pile of good compost
A wheelbarrow, shovel, and fine sifting screen
A stack of newspapers, 3-inch-high wooden boxes
With bottom slots to let them drain

A jar full of seeds you collected last year
Some others you bought at the store
Some you mail-ordered and some that you found on the floor

Loosely firm the edges of seedflats
Loosely firm the edges of seedflats
Loosely firm the edges of seedflats -- aah

Picture yourself finely sifting that
  compost
Into the wheelbarrow until it is full
Line all the boxes with two sheets of
  newspaper
So you won't lose any soil

Maybe add lime or kelp meal or rock
  dust
To the mixture you've made in the
  barrow
Fill all those seedflats with compost and
  you're almost done

Then loosely firm the edges of seedflats
  (the soil around the edges) *
Loosely firm the edges of seedflats
  (lightly press it down) *
Loosely firm the edges of seedflats (this
  keeps your flat together) * -- aah

Comments: * The Beetless apparently intended to reduce the ambiguity of the refrain by adding these three "parenthetical background comments," divergence from the Beatles' original. Any newspaper not containing heavy metals or covered with paint or other toxic materials should be safe to use as a bottom liner in flats. This "instructional" song was inspired by a gardening cartoon Jam's daughter brought home from school one day.

After pressing the edges you'll make shallow furrows
Place your seeds in them, then cover again
Water them gently, whenever they dry out
'Til you're ready to do it again

Loosely firm the edges of seedflats
Loosely firm the edges of seedflats
Loosely firm the edges of seedflats -- aah

Loosely firm the edges of seedflats
Loosely firm the edges of seedflats
Loosely firm the edges of seedflats -- aah

Loosely firm the edges of seedflats
Loosely firm the edges of seedflats (aah-ooo)
Loosely firm the edges of seedflats

The Beetless Bootleg: Great Lost Songs of the Beetless Pt. 17
96 **WHILE MY DRIP TAPE GENTLY SEEPS** (Music: WHILE MY GUITAR GENTLY WEEPS, Harrison)

An irrigation song that was never quite convincing, this may still be reworked into an irrigation song the Beetless can finally be happy with.

97 **WITH A LITTLE HELP FROM MY INTERNS** (Music: WITH A LITTLE HELP FROM MY FRIENDS, Lennon-McCartney)

Anyone familiar with the economics of small-scale organic farming will have no trouble guessing what this was about. Lyrics lost.

29
LUCKY STIFFS, THEIR LAND IS PAID

(Music: LOVELY RITA, Lennon-McCartney)

Aah!
Lucky stiffs, their land is paid
Lucky stiffs, their land is paid

Aah!
Lucky stiffs, their land is paid
How would they make it elsewise?
They'd be on the brink financially just like me

But when I think about the problem
It's not the difference in inheritance
It's our dominant false economy

Robbing Paula to pay Peter
This generation's an inheritance cheater
Spending what we got so there'll be nothing when we're through

Lucky stiffs, their land is paid
May I inquire discreetly
Do you have rich parents or did you win the lottery?

We don't pay for land destruction
Wiped out cultures, polluted water
Ozone and soil disappearing fast

Try to work with Mother Nature
And you may well end up a pauper
If you put on those farming shoes

Oh, lucky stiffs, their land is paid
Now they just have expenses
Like in the old days, living's almost free

Comments:
The Beetless rapidly transcend jealousy and covetousness, because they see the larger economic picture in which we are all disadvantaged by "our dominant false economy." Their more fortunate friends in the farming community are just that -- "lucky stiffs." The tone is almost celebratory, against the bleak backdrop of global ruin.

Lucky stiffs, their land is paid
Lucky stiffs, their land is paid
Lucky stiffs, their land is paid
Lucky stiffs, their land is paid

THE MUSIC OF THE BEATLES

Many fans know all of the Beatles' songs by heart, and will have no trouble reconstructing the background tunes for the Beetless' poetry. Others, however, may need a little help. Whichever category you fall into, we suggest you purchase a complete set of Beatles albums, listed below. They are unsurpassed in quality, and will make you glad you acquired this book (even if there's no other reason to be glad about that). Use this list in conjunction with the table of contents and the lyrics to reconstruct the tunes to your favorite Beetless poems (Beetless poem numbers follow album titles):

Please Please Me 3, 6, 16, 39, 86
With the Beatles 10, 18, 71, 88
A Hard Day's Night 14, 58, 81
Beatles For Sale 21, 32, 51, 89, 94
Help! 25, 26, 34, 40, 57, 100
Rubber Soul 22, 31, 50, 56, 72
Revolver 9, 11, 12, 20, 46, 59, 73, 85, 99
Sgt. Pepper's Lonely Heart's Club Band 8, 28, 29, 44, 62, 68, 91, 95, 97, 98
Magical Mystery Tour 2, 5, 63, 64, 65, 79, 93
The Beatles ("The White Album") 7, 17, 33, 43, 49, 53, 54, 60, 67, 69, 75, 76, 78, 82, 84, 87, 90, 96
Yellow Submarine 23, 77, 99
Abbey Road 4, 13, 15, 30, 35, 38, 41, 47, 55, 66
Let It Be 1, 24, 27, 36, 74, 80
Past Masters Vol. 1 3, 19, 45, 48, 92
Past Masters Vol. 2 1, 37, 42, 52, 61, 70, 74, 83, 87

(For a list of additional Beatles albums, see page 83.)

30
MAXWELL'S PLASTIC BUCKET

(Music: MAXWELL'S SILVER HAMMER, Lennon-McCartney)

Washing vegetables
Tool or glove receptacle
Harvest bucket, chair
Collect green weeds and take 'em to the compost pile -- i - i - ile

Fruit tree watering
Carry sifted compost in
Marker or trash can
Collecting slugs to feed 'em to ducks in a while -- i - i - ile

For storing grains and flours and beans
And relics of the past
The uses of Maxwell's plastic bucket have never been surpassed
I just wish Maxwell's plastic bucket were really built to last

Shade new transplants with
Pot up big tomatoes in
Store kelp meal and lime
Cover plants when frost is about to come -- uh uh umm

Carry animal feed
Store most any type of seed
Wash your shorts and socks
Use to prop up glass on the old cold frame -- a - a - ame

For storing raisins, crackers, or salt
Or Junior's plaster cast
The uses of Maxwell's plastic bucket have never been surpassed
I just wish Maxwell's plastic bucket were really built to last

Carry stuff anywhere
Stack 'em where there's no ladder
Water storage, bin
Use it as a soapbox or podium -- uh uh umm

Dispense rock phosphate from
Store your extra caulking gun
Pick up rusty nails
Rise bread dough or soak your infected thumb -- uh uh umm

It's better than just about any other junk
That farmers have amassed
The uses of Maxwell's plastic bucket have never been surpassed
I just wish Maxwell's plastic bucket were really built to last

> *Comments:* **New transplants** often need to be shaded from direct sun until they recover from transplant shock, which is why transplanting is usually best done in the evening. **Kelp** meal contains many trace minerals. **Cold frames** are season-extending mini-greenhouses, often placed directly over a garden bed. **Rock phosphate** is a mineral form of phosphorus, an essential plant nutrient.
>
> Rutabaga trades his drums for buckets when performing this in concert.

> The Beetless Bootleg: Great Lost Songs of the Beetless Pt. 18
> 98 **WITH YOU, WITHOUT YOU** (Music: WITHIN YOU, WITHOUT YOU, Harrison)
>
> Dating from one of Joychoi's most creative, philosophical periods, this song asked, "Is a garden without a gardener still a garden?"
>
> 99 **YELLOW ZUCCHINI** (Music: YELLOW SUBMARINE, Lennon-McCartney)
>
> Addressed the problem of overripe vegetables. The Beetless apparently decided they'd "outgrown" the childish lyric, but many fans would love to have it back.

MIGUEL

(Music: MICHELLE, Lennon-McCartney)

Miguel, Ma Bell
These are words that go together well
Poor Miguel

Miguel works on a farm
Controlled by an agribusiness monopoly
Kind of like Ma Bell

He hoes acres and acres of lettuce
Long rows of broccoli
For people he will never see
'Cause when a thing gets big
Control of it
Falls to fewer and fewer hands

Miguel, Ma Bell
How we can turn this around I can hardly tell
Mi Miguel

He's a landless descendant of farmers
Earth whispers in his ear
Can he afford to hear?
'Cause this kind of farm
Causes alarm
To every living thing

He's so blue ...

The doctor believes it is cancer
Those grapes you spray each spring
He would give anything
For the day to come
When a daughter or a son
Would be safe from such things

Comments:
This one has been denied airplay ever since it was released. The Beetless claim to have no idea why. They did make a noticeable temporary retreat from "difficult subjects" after the controversy surrounding MIGUEL.

Miguel, Ma Bell
All to put the food upon our shelves
Our own shelves

If it were up to me
I'd do it differently
Because I think about you
Mi Miguel

GARDENING WITH THE BEETLESS: QUIZ #1

Match the correct word from the second column with the phrase in the first column:

1. Loosely firm the edges of _____
2. _____ are wise
3. Human _____ are still taboo
4. Loves in all your _____
5. There's laws against _____ that grow too high
6. Collect green _____ and take 'em to the compost pile
7. _____ know where we want to be
8. _____ complement each other in nutrient and water requirements
9. Fungi feed _____, and the other way around
10. I don't need no _____, baby
11. Harvesting the _____ with bare hands is so easy
12. Use _____ not bucks
13. Dip your _____ in bleach
14. Our _____ all poison us
15. _____ are incredibulous from food that's grown at home

a. companions
b. lawns
c. wits
d. fungicides
e. supermarkets
f. tubers
g. roots
h. pruners
i. seedflats
j. tastes
k. earthworms
l. seeds
m. weeds
n. volunteers
o. turds

(for answers, see page 73)

MISTER PRUNE-RIGHT

(Music: MISTER MOONLIGHT, Roy Lee Johnson)

Mister Prune-Right

Winter and summer, come prune the trees
Remove dead wood and what's diseased
Cut off all suckers and water sprouts
Take away branches that cross or crowd

And as for all the new growth
Head it back by two-thirds
And we will love you
Mister Prune-Right

Mister Prune-Right, come again please
Thin the fruit bunches
Dip your pruners in bleach

Open center or central leader
You determine the way
Because we miss you
Mister Prune-Right

Air and sunlight penetration
Better fruiting and shape
Our trees sure need you
Mister Prune-Right
Mister Prune-Right
Mister Prune-Right

Comments: Once again making the best of adversity, the Beetless use Mister Prune-Right's absence as an opportunity to review some basic pruning theory and practice. On many trees, **winter pruning** is done to influence shape and growth, **summer pruning** to stimulate better fruiting. **Bleach** is used to sterilize pruning shears between cuts to avoid the spreading of disease. **Open center** and **central leader** are two pruning styles, in which the center of the tree is, respectively, left open or filled with a "central leader" from the main trunk.

33
MOTHER NATURE'S WON

(Music: MOTHER NATURE'S SON, Lennon-McCartney)

In every battle ever fought
Mother Nature's won
She'll grow a field of flowers through the rubble
When we're finally done

She'll cover vacant lots with grass
She'll tree our hillsides bare
She'll cleanse the air and water
As if we were never* there [*alt. version: barely]

Do do do do do do do -- do do do
Do do do do do -- do do do
Do do

When we spray her with insecticides
The insects multiply
Herbicide-resistant weeds
Crowd every roadside

Do do do do do do do do do do do
Do do do do do -- do do do
Do do do do do do -- yeah, yeah, yeah

* Our fungicides all poison us
Preservatives cause us to decay
Those survive who
Learn that peace with Her is the only way

Mmm, aah
Mother Nature's won

Comments: * The "fungicides" verse is an instrumental in the Beatles original.
 Crop loss to insect pests has increased since the advent of the chemical insecticide age, because target pests have developed pesticide resistance. A pithy testament to Nature's wisdom and Industrial Civilization's stupidity, this song posits an entirely new (but ancient) relationship between humankind and the earth. It suggests that war is a losing proposition. Most commercial radio stations didn't like this one either.

34
MULCH!

(Music: HELP!, Lennon-McCartney)

Mulch!
I need some humus
Mulch!
Just about any humus
Mulch!
Something to make into humus
Mulch!

When you were young, oh so much younger than today
You dug and tilled and left me bare to burn up in the rays
But now these days are gone, your back has gotten sore
I've closed the window you'd been crawling through, and opened up the door

Mulch me if you can with something brown
'Cause I do appreciate whatever's around
And my soil and water stay this side of town
When you deep, deep mulch me

Potatoes grow through mulch like they're in ecstacy
Harvesting the tubers with bare hands is so easy
Dark stuff helps soil warm up around tomato plants
Its deeper colors soak up sun and stain white pants

Mulch me if you can with something brown
'Cause in nature mulching systems abound
And my soil and water stay this side of town
When you deep, deep mulch me

There are some times when I don't want to be mulched, though
'Cause slugs lay eggs, and multiply, and really, really grow
When they find mulch to call a home, then go out foraging
And soils dry faster without mulch, when still wet in the spring

Mulch me if you can with something brown
'Cause I do appreciate whatever's around
Especially when the slugs are out of town
Won't you deep, deep mulch me

Mulch me, mulch me -- ooo-mmm

> *Comments:* Note the provisos in the second-to-last verse. Singing on behalf of the soil, the Beetless add a catchy tune to their "mulch" repertoire.

GARDENING WITH THE BEETLESS: QUIZ #2

Complete the statement in the first column with a verb or verb phrase from the second column:

1. 'Cause I'm 'xpected to, I _____
2. _____ if you can with something brown
3. In soils, we now know, minerals _____
4. We'd _____ inside zone one
5. She said you should never _____
6. Water gently, don't _____
7. If they _____ I'll sue
8. Devas _____ anyday
9. Some smaller seeds need to _____
10. Give plants room but please don't _____
11. It's tired of shelter, it wants to _____
12. When I've got that plot covered with paperbacks, I will _____

a. create a flood
b. beat chemicals
c. bring in leaves and compost, stuff like that
d. spray here
e. see light
f. mulch me
g. have some fun
h. clean-slate me
i. till
j. harden off
k. feed microbes
l. step on the beds

(for answers, see page 73)

OH! BARLEY

(Music: OH! DARLING, Lennon-McCartney)

Oh! barley
Wheat and millet
Rice, amaranth and quinoa
Oats, corn and buckwheat --- ooo
Rye, spelt and triticale

Oh! navy
Black and pinto
Lima, garbanzo, kidney
Fava, mung, azuki
Lentils and split peas

Peanut, pine nut -- sunflower, sesame seeds, cashew
Macadamia, chestnut and Brazil
Walnut, filbert -- acorn, almond, coco too
Pistachio, litchi, pecan, pili -- ooo -- ooo

Oh! cabbage
Carrot, lettuce
Squash, spinach, tomato
Onion, pea, corn, radish
Mint, thyme, oregano

Beet, chard, pepper -- cauliflower, leek, broccoli
Rutabaga, dill, arugula
Turnip, basil -- coriander, watercress
Nasturtium, bok choy and okra -- a-a-a-a

Oh! cherry
Apple, lemon
Pear, peach, persimmon, fig, date
Berries beyond counting
Plum, grapefruit, orange, quince, grape

Comments (OH! BARLEY): Critics didn't know what to make of this one. Were the Beetless becoming materialists? Not a single verb in the whole thing.

Comments (ONE AFTER WEST TWENTY NINE): Jam's high school French teacher required students who had committed errors to recite *"mea culpa, mea culpa, mea maxima culpa"* (Latin for I'm a bloody sinner). While helpful in some ways, elaborate bed-numbering systems are notorious for poisoning person-to-person interactions.

36
ONE AFTER WEST TWENTY-NINE

(Music: ONE AFTER NINE-O-NINE, Lennon-McCartney)

I said you'll find that lettuce in the bed after West Twenty-Nine
Just beyond the carrots, and before you reach the sign
Below the broccoli, above the peas
Directly downhill from those trees
I said you'll find that lettuce in the one after West Twenty-Nine

She said she had been looking in the bed after West Twenty-Nine
She'd peeled her eyes and she'd raked it with a comb real fine
She'd been through it once, she'd been through it twice
She thought she'd seen some baby mice
But she'd found no lettuce in the one after West Twenty-Nine

I said I made a real good system to keep these questions to a minimum
I numbered every bed East, Center, and West, so this kind of
    confusion would be addressed

I said it's clearly planted in the bed after West Twenty-Nine
We planted them real nice and we planted them in a line
I said I've come over once, I've come over twice
To spare further hassle I'll come over thrice
I swear I'll find that lettuce in the one after West Twenty-Nine

But when I got to that locality, I realized there'd been ambiguity
"After" might mean uphill or down, or to the East, and it was then I
    found ...

There was no lettuce in the bed after West Twenty-Nine
Not anywhere in sight, though I peeled my eyes real fine
I said *mea culpa* once, I said *mea culpa* twice
Mea maxima culpa, I guess I wasn't very nice
Because there is no lettuce in the bed above West ... oh
There is no lettuce in the bed below West ... oh
* There is no lettuce in the bed next to West ... oh
There is no lettuce in the one after West Twenty-Nine

> * This is an extra line tacked on to the original tune.

PAPERBACK MULCHER

(Music: PAPERBACK WRITER, Lennon-McCartney)

Paperback mulcher, paperback mulcher

Dear Sir or Madam, can you spare that book?
Do you have any more? Can I take a look?
Others use newspapers, cardboard too
But I'm a frustrated writer
So I want to be a paperback mulcher
Paperback mulcher

I will tear off the pages and soak them well
And throw them down kind of pell-mell
The edges need to overlap, I want six layers thick
This used to be lawn
But I want to be a paperback mulcher
Paperback mulcher

Paperback mulcher, paperback mulcher

When I've got that plot covered with paperbacks
I will bring in leaves and compost, stuff like that
Manure, floor sweepings, old felt hats
Layered and mixed six inches thick
Because I am a paperback mulcher
Paperback mulcher

The first year I might plant potatoes there
The second year most anything, I don't care
Cardboard or wet newspaper could do the trick as well
But my garden is me
And I want to be a paperback mulcher
Paperback mulcher

Paperback mulcher, paperback mulcher

* The weeds won't come through, you will be amazed
It takes so little work to start your gardening days
You can do this on a vacant lot or do it at a mall
You can do it almost anwhere
If you are a paperback mulcher
Paperback mulcher

If you're using cardboard, I've a tip for you
Remove staples and tape first, or when you're through
You'll be digging up metal, plastic, cellophane
For years to come ...
But I'd rather be a paperback mulcher
Paperback mulcher

Paperback mulcher, paperback mulcher

Paperback mulcher *(4x)*

Comments: * The two verses beginning with "The weeds won't come through" are "extras," tacked onto the Beatles' original tune.
   Only one or two layers are necessary when using cardboard. Be careful when gardening in areas where residues of heavy metals or other toxins may be found. This is perhaps the Beetless' most practical "mulch" song. Many listeners have followed its instructions to the letter and reaped bumper potato crops.

The Beetless Bootleg: Great Lost Songs of the Beetless Pt. 19
100 **YOU'VE GOT TO HIDE YOUR GRUB AWAY** (Music: YOU'VE GOT TO HIDE YOUR LOVE AWAY, Lennon-McCartney)

A cautionary number about labelling and securing private food stashes to protect them from human or rodent consumption. Like several others, this song proved too offensive to be either effective or appealing.

38
PERMACULTURE GARDEN

(Music: OCTOPUS'S GARDEN, Richard Starkey)

I'd like to be
Under a tree
In a Permaculture garden in the shade
Bill Mollison
Knows where we've been
In a spiral herbal garden near a glade

We would stack our functions you and me
Designing for sustainability

Complexity
Diversity
In the Permaculture garden we have made

We'd get some ducks
Use wits not bucks
Raise food with efficiency and grace
Care for the earth
Know that it's worth
Getting more familiar with our place

We'd have some fun inside zone one
No one there to tell us what to do

Plant shrubs and trees
For perennial ease
Through seas of self-sown vegetables we'd wade

Mindless toil
Destroys the soil
Not to mention spirits and backs
Observation
Cooperation
In a thriving polyculture, nothing lacks

Masanobu smiles, and Wes approves
Neighbors come and visit with us too

I'd like to be
Under a tree
In a Permaculture garden with you
In a Permaculture garden with you
In a Permaculture garden with you

> *Comments:* Bill Mollison coined the term **Permaculture** (a contraction of "permanent agriculture" and also of "permanent culture"). **Stacking functions** (performing several functions with each element) is a basic principle of Permaculture design. **Zone one** refers to the "household" zone in a Permaculture landscape (higher numbers refer to less-frequented zones, generally more distant from the house). **"Self-sown"** refers to plants which readily reseed themselves without human intervention. **Masanobu Fukuoka** has inspired many Permaculturalists with the highly productive, nearly self-maintaining polycultures he has developed in Japan, as described in *The One-Straw Revolution*, *The Natural Way of Farming*, and *The Road Back to Nature*. **Wes Jackson's** Land Institute is attempting to develop perennial polycultures ("natural systems agriculture") to replace annual grain production on our natural prairieland. The Beetless imply that these different individuals and schools are united in a common quest, in which everyone, not just the well-known "heavy hitters," can participate.

ANSWERS TO BEETLESS GARDENING QUIZZES:

#1: 1.(i.) 2.(k.) 3.(o.) 4.(l.) 5.(b.) 6.(m.) 7.(n.) 8.(a.) 9.(g.) 10.(e.) 11.(f.) 12.(c.) 13.(h.) 14.(d.) 15.(j.)

#2: 1.(i.) 2.(f.) 3.(k.) 4.(g.) 5.(l.) 6.(a.) 7.(d.) 8.(b.) 9.(e.) 10.(h.) 11.(j.) 12.(c.)

PLEASE WEED ME

(Music: PLEASE PLEASE ME, Lennon-McCartney)

Last night I said these words to my garden
I don't know how I left the kindergarten
Come on, come on, come on, come on
Please weed me, oh yeah, like I weed you

There's so much worthless stuff inside me
The valuable stuff can barely find me
Come on, come on, come on, come on
Please weed me, oh yeah, like I weed you

* My garden said to me, I hear you
But I should make this very clear to you
Some weeds -- are good -- when they're un- --
  derstood
So please weed me with care, and I'll weed you

Weeds can be good compost-makin's
Or they can keep the soil from leaving garden
  beds (garden beds)
They can be delicious too
Better than other vegetables for you
They condition soil
Good insects like 'em too

So please just selectively weed me
Give plants room but please don't clean-slate me
As for weeds -- in you -- they may be va- --
  luable too
Please weed me with care, and I'll weed you

Oh yeah, most weeds are friendly too
Oh yeah, just watch the things they do
Weed me, and I'll weed you

Comments:
* "My garden said to me" is another "extra" verse. The Beetless attempt to keep their soil protected and growing with cover-crops or "living mulches" whenever not occupied by planted vegetables, and weeds often serve this function. Once again in this song our four lads have trouble distinguishing between themselves and their garden. All for the better, we say. We learn a little about weeding too.

PREPPING DAY

(Music: YESTERDAY, Lennon-McCartney)

Prepping day
I was making Equisetum spray
Gathering materials in a special way
Oh I remember prepping day

Biodynamically
We were talking about unity
Amongst the parts of the farm family
And balance, health, and compost tea

Why we used yarrow
I don't know, but that's the way
Manure stuffed in a horn
Camomile and silica spray -- ay -- ay

Oh prepping day
We stirred 500 in a special way
We talked about what Rudolph Steiner'd say
And stopped all work when the calendar
   showed "gray"

Why we ate so much
I don't know, we got carried away
Our roots and fruits just taste too good
Next time we'll sow them on a leaf-only day --
   ay -- ay

Oh prepping day
I don't know why this song came out this way
Some laughing dancing cosmic force is at
   play
But I know devas beat chemicals any day

Mmm mmm mmm -- prepping day

Comments: This one received mixed reviews in the Biodynamic community. Pear himself was disturbed by it, as it implied less respect for **Biodynamics** that he had originally intended. This practical-spiritual approach to organic gardening and farming grew from the work of philosopher Rudolph **Steiner**, who gave a series of eight influential agricultural lectures in the 1920s. **Compost tea**, prepared by soaking finished compost in a barrel of water, is used as a liquid fertilizer. **"500"** refers to one of *(continued next page)* *(continued from previous page)* the nine basic Biodynamic preparations, which are applied to compost piles or directly to fields. **Equisetum, yarrow, manure, camomile,** and **silica** are all used in the preparation of these "**preps.**" The Biodynamic calendar specifies certain "**gray**" **days** when no work with plants should be done, due to unfavorable planetary and stellar alignments. **Devas** are believed to be plant spirits. Food at Biodynamic meetings is notoriously delicious and abundant.

41
PVC PAM

(Music: POLYTHENE PAM, Lennon-McCartney)

Well, you should see PVC Pam
Half her gadgets come from Holland or Japan
With her beds draped in plastic
Her control measures drastic
Her garden makes me wonder where I am
Yeah, yeah, yeah

She doses everything twice a day
With some fungicidal foliar spray
She mixes it herself
From seven bottles on a shelf
It's organic so it must be ok
Yeah, yeah, yeah

Comments: PVC Pam is a fictitious character. For those unfamiliar with postmodern gardening-farming techniques, **clear plastic** is frequently used as cloche material (for season extension, warmer temperatures for subtropical crops, or protection from rain), and **black plastic** as a soil-warming, weed-blocking, evaporation-inhibiting mulch. Bent pipes made of **PVC** (polyvinyl chloride) are often employed as hoop supports for plastic cloches.

42
RAINBIRD

(Music: RAIN, Lennon-McCartney)

When the rainbird comes on, they run and hide their heads
And leave the garden beds
When the rainbird comes on
When the rainbird comes on

In the summer, about an inch of water a
    week
Keeps most vegetables at their peak
Since the rain's gone
Since the rain's gone

Rainbird
You're mighty fine
Rainbird
You keep plants from dying

People tell me that for watering efficiency
Drip tape surpasses you greatly
But it's plastic
And it wears out

Rainbird
I don't mind
Rainbird
You're doing fine

When I use you, I water overnight
Not when the sun's real bright
I hand-water seeds
And plants with special needs

Heads their hide and run they on (Rainbird)
Comes the Rainbird when and leave
    (Rainbird) *(etc., and fade)*

Comments: This atypically shallow treatment of a complex subject does manage to justify the Beetless' continuing use of an overhead impact sprinkler (brand name **Rainbird**), whose advantages also include easier irrigation of seedbeds, volunteers, cover crops, and weeds; "instant-on" frost protection; and midday showers for the gardeners. In the Pacific Northwest low summertime rainfall necessitates regular irrigation. **Overnight watering** conserves water, though use of **drip tape** (drip irrigation) would conserve even more.

ROCK DUSTING SOON

(Music: ROCKY RACCOON, Lennon-McCartney)

Now somewhere in the Black Forest hills of Germany
Acid rain was killing trees fast
But in a few places, the trees seemed to thrive
These were places you could drive

It was next to road cuts
Where rock trucks had dumped their loads

Where fine rock dust from all that gravel spread there
Had blown far and wide

Rock dusting soon
Would be a great boon
To forests struggling for survival
In a world of chemicals
Rock-dust minerals
Would experience a stunning revival

In soils, we now know
Minerals feed microbes
Who turn rock into fertile topsoil
It's thousands of years of work
On a typical small rock
Unless that rock's already powder

This remineralization
Requires glaciation
That's why we think Ice Ages happen
Unless we intrude
And do what glaciers would do
To revive land that's mineral-barren

Comments: Pear had just finished reading *Secrets of the Soil* by Peter Tompkins and Christopher Bird when he wrote this one. N-P-K refers to Nitrogen, Phosphorus, and Potassium, mainstays of the reductionist chemical approach to soil science that led to chemical agriculture. Luckily that misunderstanding of soil chemistry and soil life has now been superceded, though it still informs most agricultural practice. But the Beetless don't want *(continued next page)*

N-P-K was once hot
But increasingly it's not
As we start to know soil ecosystems -- ah

Da da da da da da da da da
Da da da da da da da da da
Da da da da da da da da da da da da da da
   da
Da da do do - n - do do do
Do -- do do do do do do do do
Do -- do do do do do do do do
Do -- do do do do do do do do do do do do
   do do
Da da do do do do do do

Now rock dusting's done
On many gardens and farms
They say once in five years suffices
Vegetables grow with ease
Resist pests, decay, and disease
Are tastier and more nutritious

Ah -- now rock dusting soon
Could be a great boon
Though it pollutes and requires fossil energy
It's a byproduct I'm told
And hand-crushing would get old
And we may develop greener technology

(continued from previous page) just another "answer to everything" (rock dust) to replace the outdated one (N-P-K). They still have questions about its genesis. In fact, some rock dust is a byproduct of already-occurring rock crushing, while some is a separate, primary product. Regardless of origin, it requires transportation to its place of use (see CARRY THAT CRATE).

Oh yeah yeah
Do do do do do do do do do
Do -- do do do do do do do do
Do -- do do do do do do do do do do do do do do
Do do do do - n - do do do
Do do do do do do do do -- come on rock dust -- oh
Do do do do do do do do -- come on rock dust -- oh
Do do do do do do do do do do do do do do
The story of rock dust, use it soon

44
SALT AND PEPPER'S ONLY FOR WHEN VEGETABLES ARE BLAND

(Music: SGT. PEPPER'S LONELY HEARTS CLUB BAND,
Lennon-McCartney)

It was twenty years ago today
I started eating in a different way
Started spicing with a different style
Subtler flavors that'll make me smile
Now let me introduce to you
A fact that may arouse some fears:
Salt and pepper from my table are banned

Well, salt and pepper's only for when vegetables are bland
And that should never be the case
Salt and pepper's only for when vegetables are bland
But my garden it is no disgrace

Salt and pepper's only, salt and pepper's only, salt and pepper's only
   for food that's bland

It's wonderful to raise your own
It's certainly a thrill
Nutrition is superior
And tastes are incredibulous
From food that's grown at home

I don't really want to rock your shoe
But your diet can be something new
You can resensitize your tongue
Go from worn-out, to being young
If you wean yourself from pepper and salt
And oil-and-sugar syrup malt
You'll start to taste the beauty of the land

Comments: The Beetless pull no punches in their ode to natural flavors.

45
SHE DUG YOU

(Music: SHE LOVES YOU, Lennon-McCartney)

She dug you, yeah, yeah, yeah, she dug you, yeah, yeah, yeah
She dug you, yeah, yeah, yeah, yeah

You say you lost your tilth, well I saw it yesterday
But then she chopped you up, turned you over, you wet clay

You know she dug you, and she dug you real bad
She double-dug you, and it makes me oh so sad

She killed much soil life too, disturbed the earthworms in their homes
Displaced microbes high and low, topped you with subsoil and with stones

Because she dug you, and she dug you real bad
She double-dug you, and it makes me oh so mad -- ooo!

She dug you, yeah, yeah, yeah, she dug you, yeah, yeah, yeah
When you're dug like that, it makes me really sad

Where self-sown mustards grew is now a barren place
Perennial herbs and flowers have vanished without trace

Because she dug you, and she dug you real bad
She double-dug you, and it makes me hopping mad -- ooo!

She dug you, yeah, yeah, yeah, she dug you, yeah, yeah, yeah
When you're dug like that, it makes me really sad
When you're dug like that, it makes me really sad
When you're dug like that, it makes me really sad

Yeah, yeah, yeah
Yeah, yeah, yeah
Yeah, yeah, yeah, yeah

Comments (SHE DUG YOU):
See next page.

Comments (SHE DUG YOU, previous page): **Tilth** refers to that desirable, crumby structure in a soil that results from the activities of a healthy soil biota and sensitive cultivation practices. Responding to charges that this song is unfairly onesided, the Beetless have emphasized repeatedly that **double-digging** (which involves cultivating the soil to two spade-depths) can be beneficial in certain circumstances, when done correctly (see any of John Jeavons' books). However, they point out, it often does more harm than good. In wet clay soils, any digging can do more harm than good. This is a true story.

46
SHE SAID RAISED BED

(Music: SHE SAID SHE SAID, Lennon-McCartney)

She said
I grow all my food in raised beds
Growing food there makes me so glad
And I'm feeling I know why this technique was born

She said
All amendments go on the beds
All the water and all the care
And the path stays the same, all foot traffic goes there

She said you should never step on the beds
I said no, no, no, you're wrong, when I was a boy
I'm sure it was alright
I'm sure it was alright

She said
Get this notion into your head
You don't want to cause compaction there
Make your bed light and fluffy, not stomped and deformed

She said plants grow close together this way
Roots have downward room to spread, plants get better sun
Leaves keep sun off soil
Water loss is less

I said
I bet raised beds drain better too
In the spring they're easier to work
And the humus holds moisture when summer sets in

She said (she said)
I grow all my food in raised beds (I grow all my food in raised beds)
Growing food there makes me so glad (growing food there makes me so glad)
I grow all my food in raised beds (I grow all my food in raised beds)

Comments: As a counterbalance to SHE DUG YOU, this celebration of raised-bed gardening makes it clear that the biointensive school has much to offer. The pairing of this lyric with the tune of the Beatles' SHE SAID SHE SAID makes for an intriguing combination, highlighting the ambiguity and confusion which can occur whenever we seek truth or intimacy, whether in gardening or in love. Jam based the lyrics on a conversation he had with organic gardening icon/chef extraordinaire Pierre Fondu, during a particularly memorable party in Hollywood.

THE BEATLES: PERENNIALS

Beatles music won't die. Here are additional albums, with alternate takes and previously unheard songs, released after their breakup. We couldn't fit them into the box on page 59, but they belong there right alongside the "Big Thirteen (or Fifteen)."
Just in case you weren't paying attention, they are:

The Beatles at the Hollywood Bowl
Live at the BBC
Anthology 1   **Anthology 2**   **Anthology 3**

SHE SAID SHE COMPOSTED IN WINDROWS

(Music: SHE CAME IN THROUGH THE BATHROOM WINDOW, Lennon-McCartney)

She said she composted in windrows
Sometimes in open piles too
She never used a bin or barrel
Or a thousand-dollar Compost Zoo

Didn't anybody tell her?
Didn't anybody see?
She was flaunting with convention
She was composting for free

She said she'd always been a chancer
Tried things to see if they would work
The way she stacked those piles so pretty
Was enough to drive me near berserk

And though it was a kind of artwork
It never seemed a difficult job
She simply layered greens and browns there
Kept them moist, but not waterlogged

Didn't anybody tell her?
Didn't anybody see?
Yesterday I think I saw her
Pour on half a jar of pee
Oh yeah

Comments: A standard compost poem, in a predictably irreverent style. We feel that "she" and the Beetless have much in common. Certainly the **Compost Zoo** is equally unaffordable to all concerned. Alternating layers of **nitrogen-rich greens** and **carbon-rich browns** (with some organism-rich inoculant like manure, finished compost, or soil), in a compost pile of minimum size 4' x 4' x 4', will usually compost satisfactorily without turning. Undecomposed outside layers can be layered into a new pile. Moderate amounts of **urine** help break down the carbon in compost piles. The *Rodale Book of Composting* is a useful guide.

48
SHORT ON SALARY

(Music: LONG TALL SALLY, Enotris Johnson, Richard Penniman, Robert Blackwell)

Well he's short on salary
He's got debts up to here
He works 'til he drops
And it's getting worse each year
Oh baby, yeah baby, whoa baby, with no funds in sight

A farmer's life is ecstacy
A farmer's life is hell
If you can do without the money
You can really live quite well
Oh baby, yeah baby, whoa baby, with no funds in sight

His customers live comfortably
At fifty bucks an hour
He'd gladly pay himself twenty a day
If it were in his power
Oh baby, yeah baby, whoa baby, with no funds in sight

Well, he'd like to have some funds in sight
Have some funds in sight
Everything could be right
If he could have some funds in sight
Have some funds -- yeah, yeah, yeah, yeah, yeah

He'd like to have some funds in sight
Have some funds in sight
Everything could be right
If he could have some funds in sight
Yeah, he would have some funds -- some funds alright

Comments: The Beetless know too many overworked, underpaid farmers not to have written this song. Luckily our lads are musicians as well as gardeners-farmers, and they're going to make it big some day.

49
THINNINGS

(Music: PIGGIES, Harrison)

Have you seen the little thinnings
Lying in the dirt?
And for all the little thinnings
Life's abruptly short
Never got a chance to grow any bigger

Have you seen the bigger thinnings
These are even worse
My mom says when she pulls them out
Forever she'll be cursed
She feels such remorse for all this murder

But in their size there's nothing lacking
They don't care what size they're supposed to be
Eaten now, or eaten later
Either's a premature death if they can't seed

Everywhere there's lots of veggies
Leading shortened lives
We can have them all for dinner
No matter what their size
Thinnings can be prize for anything you're makin'

> *Comments:* "Thinnings" are plants removed from a seedflat or bed because they are growing too closely. Joychoi based this ode to thinnings on a true episode that happened with his mom.

50
THE TURD

(Music: THE WORD, Lennon-McCartney)

Chicken turds will make you free
Use horse turds and be like me
Rabbit turds I'm thinking of
Cattle turds, the word is dung
It's so fine, it's sunshine, it's a turd, dung

In the beginning, I misunderstood
But now I've got it, a turd is good

Turkey turds will make you free
Spread goat turds and be like me
Llama turds I'm thinking of
Rhino turds, the word is dung
It's so fine, it's sunshine, it's a turd, dung

Everywhere I go, I hear it said
In the good and the bad books that I have read

Compost turds, and you'll be free
You can pile them separately
Or you can layer them with plants
Green and dry, C:N balanced
It's so fine, it's sunshine, it's a turd, dung

Comments (THE TURD): We're having to hold them 'til the next page.

Now I know what animals feel must be right
Factory-farmed turds are traumatized by their plight

But with good turds your garden sings
Earthworm turds are called castings
Human turds are still taboo
But they make good compost too
It's so fine, it's sunshine, it's a turd, dung

It's a turd, dung, it's a turd, dung, it's a turd, dung, it's a turd, dung

Comments (THE TURD, previous page): Despite its overly-perfunctory treatment of the moral ambiguity of using manure from factory farms, this has become a Beetless classic. "**C:N balanced**" refers to the correct ratio of carbon to nitrogen when constructing a compost pile (about 25:1 at the outset). On composting **human turds**, see *The Humanure Handbook* by J.C. Jenkins. **Dung** is indeed sunshine, in a different form.

51
TWELVE MONTHS A YEAR

(Music: EIGHT DAYS A WEEK)

I'm a year-round garden
Yes you know it's true
And since I'm a year-round garden
You're never short of food

Hoe me, weed me
Harvest me, seed me
You'll always find something to eat here
Twelve months a year

In spring you start your transplants
Put peas right in the ground
And spuds and beans and squash and corn
'Fore summer comes around

Dig me, feed me
Water me, weed me
You'll always find something to do here
Twelve months a year

Twelve months a year
I grow food
Twelve months a year
I ask for just a little care

Summer's quite abundant
Fruit's ripest in the fall
But brassicas thrive in winter
When garlic and leeks are tall

Rake me, seed me
Mulch me, weed me
You'll always find something to plant here
Twelve months a year

Twelve months a year
I grow food
Twelve months a year
I ask for just a little care

I'd die in colder climates
But it's much milder here
I'll trade you vegetables for love
All seasons of the year

Hoe me, feed me
Harvest me, seed me
You'll always find something to eat here
Twelve months a year
Twelve months a year
Twelve months a year

> *Comments:* With its mild winters and pleasant summers, the Pacific Northwest is particularly hospitable to year-round gardens. Though the main growing season, spring-fall, requires nearly-constant presence (or a computerized watering system and helpful neighbors), the slower winter season does allow extended absence for gardeners who'd rather be either warmer or colder for a while.

52
WE CAN TURN IT 'ROUND

(Music: WE CAN WORK IT OUT, Lennon-McCartney)
(Poem: Copyright © 1997, Larry Dobberstein)

Try to see it my way
Said the organic farmer to his neighbor 'cross the road
While you see it your way
There's a chance we'll see our precious farmland all erode
We can turn it 'round, we can turn it 'round

Think of what you're saying
"Toxic sprays and poisons are the way it's always been"
Think of what I'm saying
We could save the soil and restoration could begin
We can turn it 'round, we can turn it 'round

Spray bugs all you want
They'll come a time
When pests build up immunity
I have always thought
That it's a crime
But that's not how it has to be

Try to see it my way
Common sense will tell you agribusiness is all wrong
Think about the children
How will they live if the good soil is all but gone?
We can turn it ' round, we can turn it 'round

Comments: The second of the only two "covers" the Beetless perform -- and also written (like I'M EATING GOOD FOOD) by Beetless Superfan Larry Dobberstein of Eugene, OR. For a more detailed treatment of soil erosion, see YOU'RE GONNA LOSE THAT SOIL. For the Beetless' organic paean to insect life, see BUG ME DO. For their attitude toward "weeds" and "volunteers," see PLEASE WEED ME and YOU WON'T SEED ME.

Spray weeds all you want
They'll come a time
When they build up immunity
I have always thought
That it's a crime
But that's not how it has to be

Try to see it my way
Ecocide and chemical addiction are all wrong
Think about the children
How will they live when soil and soil life's all but gone?
We can turn it ' round, we can turn it 'round

53
WHY DON'T WE DO IT WITHOUT ROADS?

(Music: WHY DON'T WE DO IT IN THE ROAD?, Lennon-McCartney)

Why don't we do it without roads?
You'd think our food it had to roll
Why don't we do it without roads?
What's gained in distance is lost in soul
No one's really stopping us
Why don't we do it without roads?

Why don't we do it without roads?
We've traded wisdom for a pot of gold
Why don't we do it without roads?
It's a way of life that's very old
We'd still be free to use walking paths
Why don't we do it without roads?

Why don't we do it without roads?
We'd then stop running over toads
We'd give the animals a place to roam
All creatures would feel more at home
It'd give us all fresh air to breathe
Why don't we do it without roads?

Comments: The Beetless tell it like it is, even as they live in degrees of compromise they must submit to in order to participate in the regeneration of Earth-based culture and the collapse of Western Civilization (or, as Gandhi might say, the lack thereof).

54
WORKDAY

(Music: BIRTHDAY, Lennon-McCartney)

You say it's your workday
Well, it's my workday too, yeah
You say you hate your workday
I can't say I do
I'm glad it's my workday
I'm happy gardening, ooo-yeah

Yes I'm having me a garden party
While you're cooped up indoors just making money
To buy stuff I'm glad I have no need for

(Workday) I would like you to dance
(Workday) Take a cha-cha-cha-chance
(Workday) You can wear these workpants
Pants! (pants!) yeah!

(Workday) I would like you to dance
(Workday) Take a cha-cha-cha-chance
(Workday) Don't look at me askance
Askance! (askance!)

You say it's your workday
Well, it's my workday too, yeah
So sorry it's your workday
I'm gonna have a good time
Try trading in your workday
When you're dead it'll be too late

Comments: Many fans have taken up the Beetless on their offer to lend out workpants. Through frequent visits to second-hand stores and garage sales, the Beetless have been able to meet the demand affordably. For a thoughtful exploration of the inner and outer work of gardening, see Jim Nollman's *Why We Garden*.

BIBLIOGRAPHY / RESOURCES PT. 1

Aprovecho Research Center, 80574 Hazelton Rd., Cottage Grove, OR 97424. Sustainable living-skills internships, publications, research.

Dr. Twisted Visits a Farm, by Kamyar Enshayan, foreword by Gene Logsdon. 1994. Available from PO Box 981, Cedar Falls, IA 50613.

Ecology Action, 5798 Ridgewood Rd., Willits, CA 95490. Biointensive gardening research and education.

Farming: A Hand Book (poems), by Wendell Berry. 1971. Harvest/Harcourt Brace Jovanovich, New York.

From the Good Earth: A Celebration of Growing Food Around the World, by Michael Ableman. 1993. Abrams, New York.

The Gift of Good Land: Further Essays Cultural and Agricultural, by Wendell Berry. 1981. North Point Press, San Francisco.

Greenward Ho!: Herbal Home Remedies — An Ecological Approach to Sustainable Health, by Tom Ward. 1990. Moby Press, PO Box 1282, Ashland, OR 97520.

How to Grow More Vegetables (Fruits, Nuts, Berries, Grains, and Others) than you ever thought possible on less land than you can imagine, by John Jeavons. 5th edition, revised, 1995. Ten Speed Press, PO Box 7123, Berkeley, CA 94707.

The Humanure Handbook: A Guide to Composting Human Manure, by Joseph C. Jenkins. 1996. Jenkins Publishing, PO Box 607, Grove City, PA 16127.

Introduction to Permaculture, by Bill Mollison with Reny Mia Slay. 1994. Tagari Publications, distributed by Permaculture Resources, PO Box 65, Califon, NJ 07830.

The Land Institute, 2440 E. Water Well Rd., Salina, KS 67401.

The Lost Valley Book of Ecological Cooking and Living. 1996. LVPC, 81868 Lost Valley Lane, Dexter, OR 97431.

(continued on page 97)

55
YOU NEVER LEND ME YOUR CRUMMY

(Music: YOU NEVER GIVE ME YOUR MONEY,
Lennon-McCartney)

You never lend me your crummy
You just sit there as my pickup falters
And in the middle of manure collection
It breaks down

You never lend me your tractor
'Cause I'm not covered by your insurance
And as you're fretting about the economy
It breaks down

Agricultural colleges
Money spent
To steal from the future
Cheat on today's rent
Biodiversity's gone
Nowhere to go

Soil and water
DNA
Air and ozone
Cultures -- hey
Progress is more important
So I'm told

But oh that magic feeling
That's in my soul
Oh that magic feeling
That's very old
That's very old

Aah-ooo
Aah-ooo
Aah-ooo

THE BEETLESS VS. THE ROLLING SCONES?

For years the press has carried reports that these two bands (one of them celebrating wholesome, organic, homegrown food, and the other going out of their way to tout food that is more "sinful") are enemies. This is absolutely not the case, though their diets do differ. The Beetless appreciate the Rolling Scones as people, as musicians, and as cooks; and vice versa. The doll on the (unreleased) *Salt and Pepper* album cover even wore a sweatshirt reading "Welcome Rolling Scones: Good Pies." Enough said.

One sweet dream
Hop on my bicycle, leave behind the limousine
Soon we're far away from here
Back to the place where cycles have their way

One sweat dream
Came true
Today
Came true
Today
Came true
Today
Yes it did, nah nah nah nah nah nah nah -- nah

One, two, three, four, five, six, seven
All good earthlings know this is heaven
One, two, three, four, five, six, seven
All good bakers save their leaven
One, two, three, four, five, six, seven
Bio-motors don't need revin'
One, two, three, four, five, six, seven
The garden's where I think I'm headin'
One, two, three, four, five, six, seven
All good earthlings ... *(repeat as above)*

> *Comments:* "**Crummy**" is slang for a beat-up old motor vehicle, in this case apparently another "beater" pickup. Kamyar Enshayan in *Dr. Twisted Visits a Farm* has eloquently lampooned **agricultural institutions** of "hire education" and research. **DNA** refers to deoxyribonucleic acid. The reference to saving **leaven** reflects the Beetless' longtime fondness for sourdough bread.

56
YOU WON'T SEED ME

(Music: YOU WON'T SEE ME, Lennon-McCartney)

If I didn't come up, you'd be enraged
But in the seed catalog, you turn the page
I volunteer all the time, I'm never hard to find
And I am growing just fine
So you won't seed me (you won't seed me)
You won't seed me (you won't seed me)

There's so much of me, you never doubt
That you'll never, ever be without
Let me tell you, hey, you don't know how long I'll stay
And there could come a day ...
Still you won't seed me (you won't seed me)
You won't seed me (you won't seed me)

Elephant garlic, calendula, kale
Parsley, chard, mustards, chickweed and Red Sails ...

Though my needs are few, my seeds are many
How 'bout gathering a few, to sow randomly
Around the garden here, maybe save some for next year
Because I think it's queer
That you won't seed me (you won't seed me)
You won't seed me (you won't seed me)

Lambsquarters, amaranth, borage, daikon
Chicory, endive, sunflowers and purslane ...

Volunteers know where we want to be
We're the best nutrition, and we grow for free
But collect our seeds, stop treating us like weeds
Or we may vanish like steeds ...
If you won't seed me (you won't seed me)
You won't seed me (you won't seed me)
Ooo -- la la la, ooo -- la la la, ooo -- la la la *(repeat and fade)*

Comments: Self-sown vegetables are also known as "**volunteers**." **Red Sails** is a variety of lettuce. Some of the Beetless' favorite vegetables and plants are listed in this memorable song, which, according to Pear, "just wrote itself."

BIBLIOGRAPHY / RESOURCES PT. 2
(continued from page 93)

Mushrooms Demystified, by David Arora. 1990. Ten Speed Press, Berkeley, CA.

The Natural Way of Farming: The Theory and Practice of Green Philosophy, by Masanobu Fukuoka. 1985. Japan Publications, New York.

The One Straw Revolution: An Introduction to Natural Farming, by Masanobu Fukuoka. 1978. Rodale Press, Emmaus, PA.

Permaculture: A Designer's Manual, by Bill Mollison. 1993. Tagari Publications, distributed by Permaculture Resources, PO Box 65, Califon, NJ 07830.

The Permaculture Activist. Subscriptions from PO Box 1209, Black Mountain, NC 28711.

Putting Food By, by Janet Greene, et. al. 1992. NAL-Dutton, New York.

The Road Back to Nature: Regaining the Paradise Lost, by Masanobu Fukuoka, Majanobu Fukuoka, and Frederic R. Metreaud. 1988. Japan Publications, New York.

The Rodale Book of Composting: Easy Methods for Every Gardener, edited by Grace Gershuny, D.L. Martin. 1992. Rodale Press, Emmaus, PA.

Secrets of the Soil, by Peter Tompkins and Christopher Bird. 1990. HarperCollins, New York.

Seed to Seed: Seed Saving Techniques for the Vegetable Gardener, by Suzanne Ashworth. 1991. Published by Seed Savers Exchange, Decorah, IA. Distributed by Chelsea Green Publishing Co., White River Junction, VT.

(continued on page 99)

57
YOU'RE GONNA LOSE THAT SOIL

(Music: YOU'RE GONNA LOSE THAT GIRL, Lennon-McCartney)

You're gonna lose that soil (yes, yes, you're gonna lose that soil)
You're gonna lose that soil (yes, yes, you're gonna lose that soil)

If you don't lay each bed out right
You're gonna lose that soil (yes, yes, you're gonna lose that soil)
Across the slope, top surface flat
Or it'll flow downhill (yes, yes, it's gonna flow downhill)

You're gonna lose that soil (yes, yes, you're gonna lose that soil)
You're gonna lose that soil (yes, yes, you're gonna lose that soil)

If you don't keep the surface covered
You're gonna have troubles (yes, yes, you're gonna have troubles)
Mulch it or keep it cover-cropped
Where there aren't vegetables (where there aren't vegetables)

You're gonna lose that soil (yes, yes, you're gonna lose that soil)
You're gonna lose that soil (yes, yes, you're gonna lose that soil)
You're gonna lose (yes, yes, you're gonna lose that soil)

Water gently, don't create a flood
 (create a flood), yeah
Or garden paths will be running
 thick with mud

(You're gonna lose that soil)
(You're gonna lose that soil)

You're gonna lose that soil (yes, yes,
 you're gonna lose that soil)
You're gonna lose that soil (yes, yes,
 you're gonna lose that soil)
You're gonna lose (yes, yes, you're
 gonna lose that soil)

Comments: Creating beds on a contour reduces erosion. **"Green manures"** are cover-crops or other plants incorporated back into the soil.
 Despite the cheerful optimism and charm that inspire such mania among their fans, the Beetless are sober realists, as they demonstrate in this cautionary number.

Grow some windbreaks, so if there's a gust (if there's a gust), yeah
You won't be seeing swirling clouds of dust

If you don't add organic matter
You will deplete it soon (you will deplete it soon)
Microbes like compost and green manures
Worms sing a happy tune (worms sing a happy tune)

You're gonna lose that soil (yes, yes, you're gonna lose that soil)
You're gonna lose that soil (yes, yes, you're gonna lose that soil)
You're gonna lose (yes, yes, you're gonna lose that soil)

BIBLIOGRAPHY / RESOURCES PT. 3
(continued from page 97)

Seeds of Change, PO Box 15700, Santa Fe, NM 87506. National organic seed company; distributor of Deep Diversity catalog, Peace Seeds Research Journals.

The Soul of Soil: A Guide to Ecological Soil Management, by Grace Gershuny and Joseph Smillie. 1996. Ag Access, PO Box 2008, Davis, CA 95617.

Start with the Soil, by Grace Gershuny. 1997. Rodale Press, Emmaus, PA.

Turning Garbage Into Gold: An Introduction to Vermiculture Biotechnology, by Uday Bhawalkar. Bhawalkar Earthworm Research Institute, Kalyani, Pune-Satara Rd., Pune -- 411 037, India.

The Unsettling of America: Culture and Agriculture, by Wendell Berry. 1977. Sierra Club Books, San Francisco.

The Western Society of Malacologists' Field Guide to the Slug, by David George Gordon. 1994. Sasquatch Books, Seattle.

What Are People For?, by Wendell Berry. 1990. North Point Press, San Francisco.

Why We Garden: Cultivating a Sense of Place, by Jim Nollman. 1994. Henry Holt, New York.

Worm Digest, quarterly, from Box 544, Eugene, OR 97440.

GLOSSARY

allelopathy: the exudation by one plant of chemicals that inhibit the growth of another plant.
"American" crops: crops originating on the American continents -- usually (but not always) frost-tender subtropicals or tropicals, from Central or South America.
antagonists: incompatible plants, either or both of which may interfere with the other's growth, health, taste, reproduction, etc..
bentonite: an absorbent aluminum silicate clay formed from volcanic ash and used to line ponds, dams, and the "homesteader's bathtub."
Biodynamics: a practical-spiritual approach to organic gardening and farming, based in the work of philosopher Rudolph Steiner.
biointensive: gardening techniques designed to maximize productivity while minimizing use of space and resources.
bioregionalism: the art of knowing, and living within the natural limits and character of, one's home place, or bioregion.
bleach: a chemical agent used to sterilize pruning shears between cuts to avoid the spreading of disease.
Brassicaceae: the cabbage family (see "mustards").
bugs: most commonly (in this context), refers to insects in general; less commonly, refers to "true bugs," a subset of that group.
C:N ratio: the ratio of carbon to nitrogen in, for example, a compost pile (where the ideal ratio is about 25:1 at the outset).
carbon-rich browns: essential elements in a compost pile.
castings: earthworm turds.
central leader: a pruning style in which a single "central leader" growing from the main trunk fills the center of the tree.
clay: fine sedimentary material, with grains smaller than 0.002 millimeters in diameter.
cloche: a mini-greenhouse, often constructed of clear plastic draped over PVC pipes (see "cold frame").
cold frame: a season-extending mini-greenhouse, often placed directly over a garden bed (see "cloche").
colloids: substances composed of many tiny particles suspended in a gel-like mass, with a high proportion of surface area to weight.
Community Supported Agriculture: a farmer-consumer partnership in which shareholders become more closely associated with a farm,

paying a yearly fee and receiving a weekly basket of various vegetables (and sometimes other foodstuffs) throughout the growing season.

companion plants: complement each other in nutrient and water requirements, growth habits, and demands for light; attract good bugs and give bad ones a fright; they can also discourage diseases, promote soil life, and keep down weeds.

compost: a mixture of decaying organic matter, often used to enrich soil and improve soil structure.

compost tea: a liquid amendment prepared by soaking finished compost in a barrel of water.

cover-crop: a crop grown specifically to protect, condition, enrich, and turn back into the soil, or to be used as compost, adding rather than subtracting organic matter in the garden or farm system.

crabgrass: any of certain grasses of the genus *Digitaria*; a troublesome perennial grass; second cousin to quackgrass.

critters: animals.

crumbs: aggregates of soil particles.

crummy: slang for a beat-up old motor vehicle, especially one used on mucky physical jobs like tree-planting.

devas: plant spirits.

digging fork: a heavy-duty fork meant for working the soil, with tines stronger than those on pitchforks and not flat like those on potato forks.

dioxins: suspected gifts, absolutely free of charge, from the industry which supplies grass seed for our golf courses and lawns.

DNA: deoxyribonucleic acid.

double-digging: any of several methods of hand-cultivating the soil to two spade-depths, described in detail in the books of John Jeavons.

drip tape: plastic irrigation line that leaks water at specific points, sometimes through "emitters"; a more durable alternative, "leaky hose," made from recycled rubber tires, seeps water all along its length.

dung: sunshine.

Equisetum: horsetail, a plant high in silica, valued for its antifungal properties.

factory farm: an animal concentration camp created to supply humans with meat, eggs, dairy and other animal products.

Five-hundred (500): one of the nine basic Biodynamic preparations.

Fukuoka, Masanobu: a Japanese rice farmer and pioneer of natural farming techniques.

garden cart: a two-wheeled alternative to the wheelbarrow, more stable and able to carry larger loads, but not able to maneuver narrow paths between beds.

garden spade: a rectangular-headed digging tool.far superior to pointy-tipped shovels for digging garden beds.

gopher plant: *Euphorbia lathyrus*, also called "mole plant."

"gray" days: days on which, according to the Biodynamic calendar, no work with plants should be done, due to unfavorable planetary and stellar alignments.

Green Gulch: a Zen Meditation Center with excellent garden soil, in Marin County, California.

green manures: cover-crops or other plants incorporated back into the soil.

hardening off: the process by which a plant is acclimated to being outdoors in the cold, wind, rain, heat, sun, etc..

humus: a brown or black organic substance resulting from the decay of vegetable or animal matter.

impact sprinkler: an overhead watering system that goes "click, click, click, click (etc.)" as it shoots off spurts of water.

inoculant, compost: any of several organism-rich materials (manure, finished compost, worm castings, soil), layered into a compost pile to facilitate its composting.

intern: (a) a student or apprentice, learning partially through practical, hands-on experience; or (b) unpaid or underpaid labor.

Jackson Wes: author, teacher, researcher, and founder of The Land Institute, which is attempting to develop perennial polycultures ("natural systems agriculture") to replace annual grain production on our natural prairieland.

jardinero: gardener (Spanish).

Jeavons, John: author, teacher, researcher, and popularizer of biointensive growing techniques.

kelp meal : a soil amendment made from seaweed, rich in trace minerals.

lime: a mineral form of calcium oxide, commonly used to reduce soil acidity (raise ph).

living mulches: cover-crops or weeds left growing where beds are not occupied by planted vegetables.

loam: a benevolent mixture of sand (large particles of disintegrated rock, often silicate), clay (fine particles), silt (intermediate-size particles), and organic matter.

malos por la salud: bad for the health (Spanish).

mea culpa, mea culpa, mea maxima culpa: "it's my fault, it's my fault, it's absolutely totally my fault" (Latin).

Mollison, Bill: author, teacher, and founder of Permaculture.

mulch: a material applied to the surface of the soil -- to provide nutrients and organic matter, to prevent evaporation of moisture, to reduce weeds, to prevent soil erosion, and/or to moderate, raise, or reduce soil temperature.

mushrooms: fruiting bodies bearing spores of fungi that live underground, bursting through duff without making a sound.

mustards: used interchangeably with "brassicas," "crucifers," and "cole crops" to indicate members of the cabbage family, Brassicaceae.

mycorrhizal fungi: keep soil rich and alive; help trees and microbes alike to survive.

N-P-K: Nitrogen, Phosphorus, and Potassium.

nitrogen-rich greens: valuable ingredients in a compost pile (food scraps and/or nitrogen-rich manures can supplement or substitute).

open center: a pruning style in which the center of the tree above the main trunk is left open.

organic matter: matter derived from living organisms.

parasites: will make live matter dead.

Permaculture: a contraction of "permanent agriculture" and also of "permanent culture"; a design system for sustainability.

pH: a measure of soil acidity, ranging from 1.0 (impossibly acid) through 7.0 (neutral) to 14.0 (impossibly basic), with most vegetables preferring a slightly acid soil (pH 6.0 to 7.0).

photosynthesis: why we are here today.

PVC: polyvinyl chloride; bent pvc pipes are often employed as hoop supports for plastic cloches.

quackgrass: *Agropyron repens*, a creeping rhizomatous grass with conspicuous white rootstalks.

radiation frosts: frosts which occur under clear night skies at air temperatures above freezing.

Rainbird: brand name of popular overhead impact sprinkler.

raised beds: garden beds that are raised above the natural level of the land -- often created by double-digging.
Red Sails: a favorite variety of red looseleaf lettuce.
Reemay: the brand name of a multi-purpose spun polyester fiber used for frost protection, heat or water retention, pest or pollinator exclusion, shade, or territorial marking.
rhizome: a horizontal stem, usually underground, which sends out roots and shoots from its nodes.
rock dust: finely ground-up rock.
rock phosphate: a mineral form of phosphorus.
rototiller: a motorized rotary cultivator and soil pulverizer.
sand: large particles of disintegrated rock, often silicate.
saprophytes: break down dead matter instead.
secaturs: the L.L. Bean of tools, a hybrid of scissors and pruning shears.
seedflats: boxes in which seeds become seedlings.
seedling: a seed that's germinated; love made manifest.
seeds: love.
self-sown: having reseeded itself (planted itself from a previous generation's seeds) without human intervention.
sheet mulching: any of several techniques of covering over existing vegetation and soil completely with a thick layer of mulch materials, then planting into or through the new layer -- or, in some cases, using the mulch mainly to smother unwanted vegetation, then moving it aside at a later date and planting into the weed-free soil below.
silt: fine sedimentary material intermediate in size between sand and clay.
soil microorganisms: microscopic and submicroscopic soil life, especially bacteria and protozoans, living at specific soil depths.
spuds: potatoes.
stacking functions: performing several functions with each element in a system -- a basic principle of Permaculture design.
Steiner, Rudolph: the Austrian philosopher whose agricultural lecture series in the 1920s inspired the development of Biodynamics.
sucker: a secondary shoot coming from the base or roots of a plant.
summer pruning: pruning done to stimulate better fruiting.
sunchokes: Jerusalem artichokes, *Helianthus tuberosus*.

symphylan: a small wormlike soil creature that feasts on organic matter and plant rootlets.

tannic acid: "a lustrous yellowish to light brown amorphous, powdered, flaked or spongy mass [or liquid form thereof] having the approximate composition $C_{76}H_{52}O_{46}$, derived from [hence contained in] the bark and fruit [and leaves] of many plants ..." (*The American Heritage Dictionary of the English Language*, 3rd edition) [additions mine].

thinnings: plants removed from a seedflat or bed because they are growing too closely.

tilth: that desirable, crumby structure in a soil that results from the activities of a healthy soil biota and sensitive cultivation practices; also, the quality of careful self-cultivation in a person.

tuber: a fleshy, swollen, usually underground stem, bearing buds or "eyes" which may give rise to new shoots.

un buen maestro: a good teacher (Spanish).

un buen patrón: a good boss (Spanish).

urine: a valuable source of nitrogen for compost piles or in the garden, when used appropriately and in moderation.

Vavilov Centers: "evolutionary hot spots" located in a narrow belt of land close to the equator, where ninety percent of the earth's vegetable life forms reputedly came into being.

vermiculture: the cultivation of earthworms (directly in the garden soil) or of manure worms (in bins or in manure or compost piles).

volunteers: self-sown vegetables; also, self-sown plants of any kind.

Ward, Tom: herbalist, wildcrafter, Permaculture instructor, appropriate-living guru, tree-house designer, and specialist in culvert maintenance.

water sprout: a rapidly growing, usually weak, vertical shoot coming off an established limb of a woody plant.

weeds: can be good compost-makin's or can keep the soil from leaving garden beds; they can be delicious too, better than other vegetables for you; they condition soil; good insects like 'em too.

windbreak: a hedge, fence, or row of trees which lessens or blocks the force of the wind.

windrow: a long row of cut hay, grain, or other vegetative or organic matter, left to dry (before being bundled) or to compost.

winter pruning: pruning done to influence shape and growth.

zone one: the "household" zone in a Permaculture landscape.

INDEX

(Numbers refer to the *Poem Number*, not the Page Number. A (c) after the poem number indicates that the term or topic is addressed in the "Comments," but not mentioned directly in the poem itself.)

acidity, soil, 13
acorns, 35
aeration, soil, 7
agribusiness, 31, 52
agrichemicals, 3, 5, 18, 31, 33, 43
agricultural economics, 20, 29, 31, 48, 84, 97
agricultural education, 55
air, 55
allelopathy, 73
almonds, 35
amaranth, 35, 56
American crops, Central and South, 25
American crops, North, 9
animals, 1, 10, 15, 17, 22, 50, 53, 58, 69, 73, 77
animals, feeding of, 30
antagonists, 26
apples, 35
arugula, 13, 35
asparagus, 26
azuki beans, 35
Baja California, 5
barley, 35
basil, 25, 35
beans, 9, 25, 26, 30, 35, 51
bed formation, on contour, 57
bed numbering, 36
bees, 16, 59
beets, 26, 35
beneficial insects, 3, 26, 39

bentonite, 14
berries, 35
Berry, Wendell, 61
Bhawalkar, Uday, 7(c)
biodiversity, 2, 9(c), 12, 38, 55
biodynamics (Biodynamics), 40, 62
biointensive planting, 26, 46, 62
bioregionalism, 51, 53, 91
birds, 16, 73
black beans, 35
blackberries, 63
bleach, 32
blights, 9(c)
blueberries, 9
bok choy, 13, 35
bones, 13
borage, 56
brassicas (Brassicaceae), 13(c), 51
broccoli, 10, 13, 22, 31, 35, 51
brown(s), 34, 47
bucket, slug, 15, 30
buckets, plastic, 30
buckwheat, 35
bugs, 3, 26, 39, 52
bullfrogs, 77
C:N ratio, 50
cabbage, 10, 26, 35, 90
calcium, 13
calendar, biodynamic, 40
camomile, 26, 40
cannery waste, 23
canning, 18
carbon, 47(c), 50
cardboard, 23, 37
carrots, 10, 22, 25, 26, 35, 36
cashews, 35
castings, earthworm, 50
cats, 1
cattle, as manure source, 50
cauliflower, 35
central leader, 32
Chadwick, Alan, 62, 63
chard, 35

cherries, 35
chestnuts, 35
chickens, 22, 50
chicory, 56
clay, 14, 45
cloches, plastic, 41
clover, 27
coconuts, 35
cold frames, 30
cole crops, 13(c)
collards, 13
colloids, 17
Community Supported Agriculture (CSA), 20(c), 67
compaction, soil, 17, 19, 46, 71
companion planting, 26
complexity, 38
compost, 20, 27(c), 28, 30, 37, 39, 47, 50, 57, 66
compost tea, 40
cooperation, 38
coriander, 35
corn, 9, 25, 26, 35, 51
cover-crops, 39, 57
crabgrass, 27
cranberries, 9
crates, 4
cress, 13
cross-cultural perspectives, 5, 8, 29, 31
crucifers, 13(c)
crumbs, 14
crummy, 55
cucumbers, 26
cultivation, 10(c), 17, 19, 34, 45
cultural extinction, 29, 55
cycles, 55
daikon (radish), 56
dates, 35
decay, 43
deer, 73
devas, 40
diet, 13, 18, 22, 39, 44, 83, 86

dieter's potatoes, 9
digging, 19, 34, 45, 51, 80
dill, 26, 35
diseases, plant, 26, 32(c), 43, 73
ditches, 5, 14
diversity, 38
DNA, 55
double-digging, 45
Dr. Twisted Visits a Farm, 55(c)
drainage, 10(c), 27, 46, 92
drip irrigation, 42, 96
drip tape, 42, 96
dry materials, for compost, 50
dryland farming, 5, 6
ducks, 38
dung, 23, 50
early plantings, 24
earthworm castings, 50
earthworms, 7, 17, 45, 50, 57
economics, agricultural, 20, 29, 48, 84, 97
economics of land ownership, 29, 87
egg shells, 13
eggplants, 25
elephant garlic, 56
endive, 56
Equisetum, 40
erosion, soil, 27, 29, 39, 52, 55, 57
exotics, 77
factory farms, as manure source, 50
fall, 21, 51
farmers markets, 20
farming, 29, 79
favas, 35, 78
felines, 1
fennel, 26
fertility, soil, 7, 43, 57
figs, 35
fish, 5, 22
Five-hundred (500), 40
floor sweepings, 37

flowers, 5, 16, 24, 33, 45
Fondu, Pierre, 28(c)
food, fast, 18
food, junk, 22
food preservation, 18, 89, 100
food preservatives, 33
food scraps, 23
food storage, 100
fork, digging, 18
freezing, 18
French Intensive, 62
From the Good Earth, 5(c)
frost protection, 25, 30
frosts, 25, 30
frosts, radiation, 25
fruit trees, 5, 30, 32
fruits, 35, 40, 51
Fukuoka, Masanobu, 38
fungi, 21
fungicides, 33
fungicides, organic, 41
gadgets, 41
garbanzo beans, 35
garden cart, 4
garden siting, 92
gardener, role of, 98
garlic, 26, 51
garlic, elephant, 56
genetic heritage, 2, 9(c), 73
goats, as manure source, 50
golf courses, 12
gopher plant, 10(c)
gophers, 10, 73
grains, 22, 24, 30
grapefruit, 35
grapes, 16, 31, 35
grass, 12, 17, 27, 33
grass clippings, 23
grass seed industry, 12
Green Gulch Zen Center, 14
green manures, 57
greenhouses, 24, 75
greens, 13, 47, 50

hardening off, 24
harvesting, 11, 18, 20, 30, 34, 51, 80, 85
hay, rotten, 23, 64
health (and diet), 22, 39
heavy metals, 28(c), 37(c)
herbalists, 1(c), 11(c), 16
herbicides, 33, 52
herbs, 5, 16, 38, 45
hoeing, 51
homegrown food, 12, 44, 83
horses, as manure source, 50
How to Grow More Vegetables ..., 26(c)
humans, as manure source, 50
Humanure Handbook, The, 50
humus, 14, 34, 46
hybrid varieties, 9(c)
Ice Ages, 43
identity, 8, 79, 98
impact sprinklers, 42
imported crop varieties, 9(c)
injuries, 27, 34, 38, 65, 95
insecticides, 3, 33, 52
insects, 3, 33, 52, 73
interns, 97
irrigation, 5, 42, 51, 57, 69, 96
irrigation for frost protection, 25
irrigation of compost piles, 47
irrigation of seedflats, 28
irrigation requirements, 26, 42, 73
Jackson, Wes, 38, 61
Jeavons, John, 26(c)
Jerusalem artichokes, 9(c)
junk, 30
junk food, 22
kale, 10, 13, 26
kelp meal, 28, 30
kidney beans, 35
knife, alternatives to, for harvesting, 11
labor, manual, 4, 19, 38, 43, 54
lambsquarters, 56

land destruction, 29
land distribution, 87
Land Institute, The, 38
land stewardship, 5, 38
lawns, 12, 37
leaf crops, 24, 40
leaves, 23, 37
leeks, 35, 51
legumes, 27(c), 35
lemons, 35
lentils, 35
lettuce, 26, 31, 35, 36
Liebig, J., 88
lima beans, 35
lime, 13, 27, 28, 30
litchi nuts, 35
llamas, as manure source, 50
loam, 14
manual labor, 4, 19, 38, 43, 54
manure, 23, 37, 40, 47(c), 50, 55, 94
marigolds, 26
markets, 84
markets, farmers, 20
meadows, 12, 16
meat, 12, 22
medicinal plants, 11, 16
melons, 85
microorganisms (microbes), 7, 17, 21, 43, 45
millet, 35
minerals, 13, 45
mints, 26, 35
Mollison, Bill, 38
money, 20, 29, 38
Mother Nature, 29, 33
mulch, 14, 23, 34, 37, 51, 57
mulch, living, 39(c)
mung beans, 35
mushrooms, 21
Mushrooms Demystified, 21(c)
mustard family, 13
mustards, 13, 45

mycorrhizal fungi, 21
N-P-K, 43
nasturtiums, 26, 35
native crops, 9
native species, 12, 77
natives vs. exotics, 77
Nature, Mother, 29, 33
navy beans, 35
newspapers, 28, 37
nitrogen, 43(c), 47(c)
nitrogen fixation, 27(c)
North American crops, 9
nutrient requirements, 26
nutrients, soil, 14, 21, 73
nutrition, 44, 56 (see also diet)
oak leaves, 13
oats, 35
observation, 38
okra, 35
old felt hats, 37
onions, 26, 35
open center, 32
oranges, 35
oregano, 35
organic farming, 52
organic matter, 23, 57
overripe vegetables, 99
ozone depletion, 29
paints, 28(c)
paper, 23
paperbacks, 37
parasites, 21
parsley, 10, 26
parsnips, 10
pasta, 22
paths, garden, 27, 46, 57
peaches, 35
peanuts, 35
pears, 35
peas, 26, 35, 36, 51, 78
peas, split, 35
pecans, 35
pee (urine), 47

pepper, 44
peppermint, 26
peppers, 25, 35
perennials, 38, 45
Permaculture, 38
persimmons, 35
pesticides, 52 (see also herbicides, insecticides, fungicides)
pests, 1, 10, 26, 34, 43, 52, 58, 69, 77
pH, soil, 13, 73
phosphate, rock, 30
phosphorus, 43(c)
photosynthesis, 68
pickup trucks, 4, 55
pigs, 22, 23
pili nuts, 35
pine nuts, 35
pinto beans, 35
pistachios, 35
plastic buckets, 30
plums, 35
pollination, 3
polycultures, 26, 38
potassium, 43(c)
potatoes, 9, 10, 25, 34, 37, 51, 80
preparations ("preps"), biodynamic, 40
preservation, food, 18, 89, 100
preservatives, food, 33
progress, 55
pruning, 32
purslane, 56
Putting Food By, 18(c)
PVC, 41
quackgrass, 17
quinces, 35
quinoa, 35
rabbits, 50, 73, 74
radiation frosts, 25
radishes, 26, 35 (see also daikon)
Rainbirds, 42
raised beds, formation of, 46, 57

raisins, 30
redistribution, land, 87
Reemay, 25
remineralization, 43
rhinos, as manure source, 50
rhizomatous grasses, 27(c)
rice, 35
roads, 53
rock dust, 28, 43
rock phosphate, 30
Rodale Book of Composting, The, 47
rodents, 1(c), 69, 100 (see also gophers)
root cellars, 18, 89
root crops, 24, 40
rototillers, 19
rutubagas, 35
rye, 35
salt, 44
sand, 14
Santa Cruz, 62
saprophytes, 21
sea cabbage, 13
season extension: see cloches, cold frames, greenhouses, mulch
secaturs, 16
Secrets of the Soil, 43(c)
seed beds, 1, 10(c), 42(c), 57
seed depth, 2, 6
seed flats, 28
seed saving, 2, 24, 27, 56
seed size, 6
seed sowing, 2, 28, 51, 56, 81, 82
seed starting, 2, 28, 51, 56, 81, 82
seed storage, 30, 81
Seed to Seed, 2(c)
seedcrops, 24
seedlings, 24, 26
seeds, 2, 28, 56
self-sown (volunteer) vegetables, 38, 42(c), 45, 56
sesame seeds, 35
sheet mulching, 37

sheets, as frost protection, 25
shelf life, crop, 43
shovels, 5, 28
shrubs, 38
sifting soil, 28
silica spray, 40
siting, garden, 92
slugs, 15, 34, 58, 73
snakes, 17
soil, 14, 17, 19, 34, 47(c), 57
soil, barren, 34, 45
soil chemistry, modern approach to, 43(c), 88
soil compaction, 17, 19, 46, 71
soil conditioning, 39
soil conditions, 92
soil ecology and soil life, 7, 17, 19, 26, 43, 45, 52
soil erosion, 27, 29, 39, 52, 55, 57
soil nutrient depletion, 57
soil stabilization, 27(c), 33, 34, 39, 57
Soul of Soil, The, 17(c)
spade, garden, 15, 19
spelt, 35
spices, 44
spinach, 26, 35
split peas, 35
spring, 15, 51
spuds (potatoes), 9, 26, 51
squash, 9, 35, 51
stacking functions, 38, 74
Steiner, Rudolph, 40
stones, 45
straw, 23
strawberries, 26
subsoil, 45
suburbanites, 8, 12
summer, 51
sun, 76
sun angle, 92
sun, lack of, 73
sun on soil, 34, 46

sun-drying food, 18
sunchokes, 9
sunflowers, 9, 35, 56
supermarkets, 18
sustainability, 38
symbiosis, 21, 26
symphylans, 73
synergism, 74
tannic acid, 13(c)
technology, 43, 93 (see also tools, tractors, transportation)
thinnings, 49
thyme, 35
tillage, 17, 19, 34
tilth, 45
toads, 53
tofu, 22
tomatoes, 9, 25, 26, 30, 34, 35
tool care, 8, 93
tool repair, 8
tools, 4, 8, 11, 17, 19, 30, 32, 41
topsoil formation, 43
toxins, 28(c), 37(c), 52
tractors, 19, 55, 72
transplanting, 24, 26, 30, 36, 51
transportation (materials and foodstuffs), 4, 20, 43, 53, 60, 72
traps, gopher, 10
tree frogs, 77
trees, 21, 32, 33, 36, 38, 43
triticale, 35
turds, 50, 94 (see also manure)
turnips, 26, 35
ultraviolet radiation, 73
urban settlement, 9(c)
urbanites, 8
urine (pee), 47
Vavilov Centers, 9(c)
vegetable washing, 30
vegetables, overripe, 99
vermiculture, 7
vinefruits, 24

vitamins, 13
volunteer (self-sown) vegetables, 38, 42(c), 45, 56
Ward, Tom, 11
water conservation, 34, 46
water pollution, 29, 55
water storage, 30
watercress, 35
watering: see irrigation
weather and seasons, 24, 25, 51, 73
weeding, 51
weeding, selective, 39
weeds, 17, 26, 30, 33, 37, 39, 52
wheat, 35
wheelbarrows, 4, 28
Why We Garden, 54(c)
wild vegetables, 9, 16, 39
wildcrafting, 11, 16, 21
windbreaks, 57
winter, 15, 51
work, 54
workpants, 54
Worm Digest, 7(c)
worms, 7, 57
yard waste, 23
yarrow, 40
year-round gardening, 51, 78
zone one, 38
zucchini, 99

Reviews and Current Info.:
http://members.aol.com/growseed

ORDERING INFORMATION

Additional copies of *The Beetless Gardening Book: An Organic Gardening Songbook / Guidebook* are available from your bookseller, or direct from Carrotseed Press for $10.95 postpaid (check or money order). Generous bulk discounts are also available -- please write us for rates. Our address:

Carrotseed Press
PO Box 1174
Cottage Grove, OR 97424

Please send us your address (and comments, if any) if you enjoyed this book and would like to hear of any future publications by Carrotseed Press or the Beetless. We promise not to mulch with any fan mail.